W0010197

NORTHSTAR 2
READING & WRITING
FOURTH EDITION

Authors   NATASHA HAUGNES

BETH MAHER

Series Editors   FRANCES BOYD

CAROL NUMRICH

Dedication

Charlie, Emmet, Oliver, Niko, Toby, and Theo.

NorthStar: Reading & Writing Level 2, Fourth Edition

Copyright © 2015, 2009, 2004, 1998 by Pearson Education, Inc.

All rights reserved.

No part of this publication may be reproduced, stored in a retrieval system,
or transmitted in any form or by any means, electronic, mechanical,
photocopying, recording, or otherwise, without the prior permission of the publisher.

Pearson Education, 10 Bank Street, White Plains, NY 10606

Staff credits: The people who made up the **NorthStar: Reading & Writing Level 2, Fourth Edition** team,
representing editorial, production, design, and manufacturing, are Kimberly Casey, Tracey Cataldo,
Rosa Chapinal, Aerin Csigay, Mindy DePalma, Dave Dickey, Nancy Flaggman, Niki Lee, Françoise Leffler,
Amy McCormick, Mary Perrotta Rich, Robert Ruvo, Christopher Siley, and Debbie Sistino

Text composition: ElectraGraphics, Inc.
Editorial Services: Lakeview Editing Services, LLC, and Scribble Creative, LLC

Library of Congress Cataloging-in-Publication Data

Haugnes, Natasha, 1965–
  Northstar 2 : Reading and writing / Authors: Natasha Haugnes, Beth Maher. — Fourth Edition.
      pages cm
  ISBN-13: 978-0-13-338216-7 (Level 2) – ISBN 978-0-13-294039-9 (Level 3) – ISBN 978-0-13-338223-5
(Level 4) – ISBN 978-0-13-338224-2 (Level 5)
1. English language—Textbooks for foreign speakers. 2. Reading comprehension—Problems,
exercises, etc. 3. Report writing—Problems, exercises, etc. I. Maher, Beth, 1965- II. Title. III.
Title: Northstar two. IV. Title: Reading and writing.
  PE1128.H394 2015
  428.2'4—dc23

                                                                              2013050584

Printed in the United States of America

ISBN 10: 0-13-404975-6 (International Edition)
ISBN 13: 978-0-13-404975-5 (International Edition)

5   18

CONTENTS

WELCOME TO
NORTHSTAR

A BLENDED-LEARNING COURSE FOR THE 21ST CENTURY

Building on the success of previous editions, *NorthStar* continues to engage and motivate students through new and updated contemporary, authentic topics in a seamless integration of print and online content. Students will achieve their academic as well as language and personal goals in order to meet the challenges of the 21st century.

New for the FOURTH EDITION

★ Fully Blended MyEnglishLab
NorthStar aims to prepare students for academic success and digital literacy with its fully blended online lab. The innovative new MyEnglishLab: *NorthStar* gives learners immediate feedback— anytime, anywhere—as they complete auto-graded language activities online.

★ NEW and UPDATED THEMES
Current and thought-provoking topics presented in a variety of genres promote intellectual stimulation. The authentic content engages students, links them to language use outside of the classroom, and encourages personal expression and critical thinking.

★ EXPLICIT SKILL INSTRUCTION and PRACTICE
Language skills are highlighted in each unit, providing students with systematic and multiple exposures to language forms and structures in a variety of contexts. Concise presentations and targeted practice in print and online prepare students for academic success.

★ LEARNING OUTCOMES and ASSESSMENT
A variety of assessment tools, including online diagnostic, formative and summative assessments, and a flexible gradebook, aligned with clearly identified unit learning outcomes, allow teachers to individualize instruction and track student progress.

THE NORTHSTAR APPROACH TO CRITICAL THINKING

What is critical thinking?

Most textbooks include interesting questions for students to discuss and tasks for students to engage in to develop language skills. Often these questions and tasks are labeled critical thinking. Look at this question as an example:

When you buy fruits and vegetables, do you usually look for the cheapest price? Explain.

The question may inspire a lively discussion with students exploring a variety of viewpoints—but it doesn't necessarily develop critical thinking. Now look at another example:

When people in your neighborhood buy fruits and vegetables, what factors are the most important: the price, the freshness, locally grown, organic (without chemicals)? Make a prediction and explain. How can you find out if your prediction is correct? This question does develop critical thinking. It asks students to make predictions, formulate a hypothesis, and draw a conclusion—all higher-level critical thinking skills. Critical thinking, as philosophers and psychologists suggest, is a sharpening and a broadening of the mind. A critical thinker engages in true problem solving, connects information in novel ways, and challenges assumptions. A critical thinker is a skillful, responsible thinker who is open-minded and has the ability to evaluate information based on evidence. Ultimately, through this process of critical thinking, students are better able to decide what to think, what to say, or what to do.

How do we teach critical thinking?

It is not enough to teach "about" critical thinking. Teaching the theory of critical thinking will not produce critical thinkers. Additionally, it is not enough to simply expose students to good examples of critical thinking without explanation or explicit practice and hope our students will learn by imitation.

Students need to engage in specially designed exercises that aim to improve critical thinking skills. This approach practices skills both implicitly and explicitly and is embedded in thought-provoking content. Some strategies include:

- subject matter that is carefully selected and exploited so that students learn new concepts and encounter new perspectives.
- students identifying their own assumptions about the world and later challenging them.
- activities that are designed in a way that students answer questions and complete language-learning tasks that may not have black-and-white answers. (Finding THE answer is often less valuable than the process by which answers are derived.)
- activities that engage students in logical thinking, where they support their reasoning and resolve differences with their peers.

Infused throughout each unit of each book, *NorthStar* uses the principles and strategies outlined above, including:

- Make Inferences: inference comprehension questions in every unit
- Vocabulary and Comprehension: categorization activities
- Vocabulary and Synthesize: relationship analyses (analogies); comparisons (Venn diagrams)
- Synthesize: synthesis of information from two texts teaches a "multiplicity" approach rather than a "duality" approach to learning; ideas that seem to be in opposition on the surface may actually intersect and reinforce each other
- Focus on the Topic and Preview: identifying assumptions, recognizing attitudes and values, and then re-evaluating them
- Focus on Writing/Speaking: reasoning and argumentation
- Unit Project: judgment; choosing factual, unbiased information for research projects
- Focus on Writing/Speaking and Express Opinions: decision making; proposing solutions

THE NORTHSTAR UNIT

1 FOCUS ON THE TOPIC

* **CT** Each unit begins with a photo that draws students into the topic. Focus questions motivate students and encourage them to make personal connections. Students make inferences about and predict the content of the unit.

MyEnglishLab

CT A short self-assessment based on each unit's learning outcomes helps students check what they know and allows teachers to target instruction.

---

*indicates Critical Thinking

Two contrasting, thought-provoking readings, from a variety of authentic genres, stimulate students intellectually.

CT Students predict content, verify their predictions, and follow up with a variety of tasks that ensure comprehension.

CAN WE TEACH CREATIVE THINKING IN SCHOOLS?
By Martha Maddux

*Steve Jobs **created** the iPod.*

Lady Gaga writes hit songs.

Mom made a delicious dinner with the food she found in the refrigerator.

Uncle Fred fixed our broken car with a can opener.

Lady Gaga

1 These creative people all did important things. Some people were famous and they changed history; others were not well known and they only helped one family for a day.

2 None of the people on the list finished college. Many of the world's most creative thinkers learned t[...] school.

3 Creative thinki[...] It helps us make [...] solve everyday pr[...] easy answer. Yet tr[...] **encourage** creati[...] don't know how [...]

5 In contrast, creative thinking results in **original** answers—new answers that others don't usually think of. 2 + 2 = 4 if you are counting houses or apples. But if a student is counting 2 hungry foxes[1] + 2 fat chickens, then 2+2 = 2 happy foxes.

6 Most people think creative thinking is difficult to understand. They think it is hard to teach. They think they can't measure or grade it. But it is not so complicated. Creative thinking is putting different ideas together in new ways.

7 Some skilled teachers teach creative thinking all the time, in addition to teaching facts. They might teach students to measure the size of a room and also have them describe the size of a room ("It's the size of a racquetball court"; Or [...]

Tips for Success in College: How to Be Creative

1 As you begin college, you will receive lots of advice about how to be a good student; for example, always attend your classes, be organized, and get to know your teachers. This is all great advice, and it will certainly help you to succeed in your classes. But there is another kind of advice that is less common: advice to help you *use* what you learn in your classes to make something new and original!

2 The following tips may be the most important ones that you get: Tips on how to be creative.

Be curious

3 This is the most important tip, and there are so many ways to do it: If you walk the same way to school every day, take another path. List three classes that you don't know anything about at your school. Then take one. When your roommate invites you to a cricket match, say "YES!" Even if you don't know anything about cricket, go and learn about it. Being **curious** helps us learn new things. The more things we know about,

A cricket match

CONNECT THE READINGS

STEP 1: Organize

Look at Reading One (**R1**) and Reading Two (**R2**) again. Choose phrases from the list to complete the chart. The example answer is the only one that uses a phrase twice.

- take risks
- whatever you create, make a lot of it
- logical thinking and facts
- helps us make new things [and] solve everyday problems that don't have one easy answer
- college students
- be curious
- schools
- teach creative thinking
- combining ideas in new ways
- help you use what you learn in your classes to make something new and original

	READING ONE (R1)	READING TWO (R2)
1. Definition of creative thinking	combining ideas in new ways	combining ideas in new ways
2. Opposite of creative thinking		
3. Why is creative thinking important?		
4. Who or what needs to change?		
5. What should they do?	teach creative thinking	a. _____ b. _____ c. _____

STEP 2: Synthesize

Use ideas from the chart above, as well as your own ideas, to complete the conversation between Kristin and Joshua, two engineering students.

JOSHUA: My design class is making me crazy. I think I'm going to drop it.

KRISTIN: But you are an engineering major! You have to take design.

JOSHUA: I know. But I don't understand what Professor Sousa wants me to do. I'm getting lots of Cs.

(continued on next page)

Creative Thinking **37**

CT Students are challenged to take what they have learned and organize, integrate, and synthesize the information in a meaningful way.

MyEnglishLab

Vocabulary Practice

Choose the correct words to complete the paragraphs.

1 MC Escher was a very creative artist. His pictures look ordinary at first. But when you look closer, you can see that they are often not logical. For example, one famous picture has a stairway that only goes in a circle. It looks like it just goes up, but that is not possible! His drawings are so original. I have never seen any others like them. I am very [____▼____] about how he makes these interesting drawings, so I just bought a book about him.

2 Dr Clarion is a really interesting professor. He is a scientist and an artist. He thinks that [____▼____] science and art is really interesting. For example, last year he did a project about pollution in a local river. He gathered lots of facts about the river. And when he was done with the scientific [____▼____], he painted several [____▼____] about the river. He took his paintings to a big scientific meeting and talked about them there. He loves [____▼____].

Submit

Copyright © 2013 Pearson Education Limited | Pearson Education | www.myenglishlab.com | Terms and conditions | Cookie policy | Credits

ALWAYS LEARNING   PEARSON

MyEnglishLab

Auto-graded vocabulary practice activities reinforce meaning and pronunciation.

EXPLICIT SKILL INSTRUCTION AND PRACTICE

DETAILS

Cross out the incorrect ending to each statement.

1. Creative skills are important because _____.
   a. they help us make new things
   b. they help us solve everyday problems
   c. they help us learn math better

2. Schools often don't teach creative thinking because _____.
   a. students don't want to learn creative thinking
   b. teachers don't know how to teach it
   c. creative thinking is difficult to measure

3. Creative thinking _____.
   a. is impossible to understand
   b. is putting ideas together in new ways
   c. results in original answers

4. Creative thinking questions _____.
   a. usually have one correct answer
   b. have many possible answers
   c. ask you to put information together in new ways

CT Step-by-step instructions and practice guide students to exercise critical thinking and to dig deeper by asking questions that move beyond the literal meaning of the text.

MAKE INFERENCES

INFERRING CONNECTIONS BETWEEN GENERAL STATEMENTS AND EXAMPLES

An **inference** is an educated guess about something that is not directly stated in the text. Writers often use examples to help readers understand a general statement. Sometimes readers need to **infer** the connection between a general statement (or definition) and an example in a text.

Look at the general statement and example and read the explanation.

- **General statement:** Creative thinking is putting different ideas together in new ways.
- **Example:** It's [the room is] the size of a racquetball court. *(paragraph 7)*

In this example of creative thinking, the student puts different ideas together in new ways: He describes the size of a room by putting together his knowledge of math and sports.

After reading the example closely, we can **infer** its connection with the general statement, and we get a better understanding of what creative thinking is.

UNIT 2

READING SKILL

1. Read paragraph 3 of Reading Two again. The title of that paragraph is "Be curious." How many examples of specific ways to be curious can you find in that paragraph? Underline them.

RECOGNIZING EXAMPLES

Examples help readers understand the general idea in a text. Usually in English, the writer gives the general idea (statement) first, then the specific examples. Sometimes the writer introduces examples with the words *for example*.

General statement:
- Be curious.

Specific examples:
- If you walk the same way to school every day, take another path.
- List three classes you know nothing about at your school. Then take one.
- When your roommate invites you to a cricket match, say "YES!"

2. Read paragraphs 4 and 5 of Reading Two again. Each paragraph has a general statement and several examples. Write them in this e-chart.

Paragraph 4

general statement	example 1
	example 2
	example 3

Paragraph 5

general statement	example 1
	example 2
	example 3

Now discuss these questions with a partner.

1. How many examples are in each paragraph?
2. Do they help you understand the general statement?

GO TO MyEnglishLab FOR MORE SKILL PRACTICE.

36   UNIT 2

Explicit skill presentation and practice lead to student mastery and success in an academic environment.

MyEnglishLab

Key reading skills are reinforced and practiced in new contexts. Meaningful and instant feedback provides students and teachers with essential information to monitor progress.

Reading Skill: Recognizing Examples

Read the article. Choose all the answers that match the category.

City College Counseling Center
Student Success Workshop
- Do you feel like you don't have enough time to finish all of your daily tasks and assignments?
- Do you spend a lot of time studying but still get poor grades?
- Do you have trouble concentrating in classes and lectures?
- Do you delay doing your school work and put off your assignments until just before they are due?

If you answered "yes" to any of these questions, then this College Success Workshop is for you! There are many factors that lead to student success, such as choosing the right classes, having good study skills, getting help from teachers and counselors, and staying healthy and active. Another important factor is time management. Many students don't know how to manage their time well. For example, do you try to multitask, or do other activities when you study, such as texting friends while you do homework? You may think you are saving time, but in fact multitasking actually has a negative effect on your ability to think and learn. Many research studies show that our brains are not able to concentrate on more than one challenging task at a time. Studies also show that students who multitask do worse in school than students who don't. They take more time to finish their work, and they receive lower test scores and grades.

1   Examples of four factors that lead to student success are:
   - [ ] spending a lot of time studying but still getting poor grades
   - [ ] choosing the right classes
   - [ ] having good study skills
   - [ ] getting help
   - [ ] staying healthy
   - [ ] trying to multitask

2   Three examples of ways students don't manage time well are:
   - [ ] choosing the right classes
   - [ ] trying to multitask
   - [ ] doing other activities while studying
   - [ ] texting friends

3 FOCUS ON WRITING

Productive vocabulary targeted in the unit is reviewed, expanded upon, and used creatively in this section and in the final writing task. Grammar structures useful for the final writing task are presented and practiced. A concise grammar skills box serves as an excellent reference.

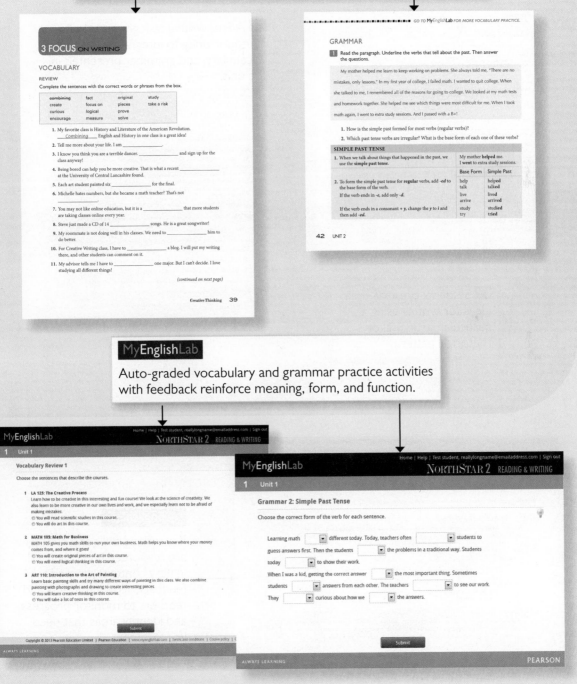

MyEnglishLab

Auto-graded vocabulary and grammar practice activities with feedback reinforce meaning, form, and function.

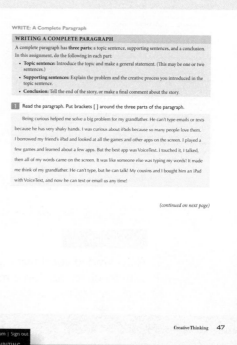

FINAL WRITING TASK

In this unit, you read about the differences between creative thinking and logical thinking. You also read some suggestions for how to be creative.

Now you are going to **write a paragraph about a time you (or someone you know) used creative thinking to solve a problem.** Introduce the story. Describe the problem. Tell how you (or someone else) used creative thinking (being curious, combining ideas, taking risks, making a lot of something) to solve it. Use the vocabulary and grammar from the unit.*

PREPARE TO WRITE: Charting a Writing Prompt

Charting your writing prompt can help you make sure you answer all the parts of a question when you write. The chart below has one row for each part of the question you will answer in your paragraph.

1. Introduce the story	Being curious helped me solve a big problem for my grandfather.
2. Describe the problem	My grandfather can't type emails or texts because he has very shaky hands.
3. Tell how you (or someone else) used creative thinking (being curious, combining ideas, taking risks, making a lot of something) to solve it.	I was curious about iPads because so many people love them. I found the VoiceText app. It made me think of my grandfather.

Look at the chart and think about a time you or someone else used creative thinking to solve a problem. The problem might be a difficult assignment in school, or it might be an everyday problem. Complete the chart. Then discuss your answers with a partner.

1. Introduce the story	
2. Describe the problem	
3. Tell how you (or someone else) used creative thinking (being curious, combining ideas, taking risks, making a lot of something) to solve it.	

_____
* For Alternative Writing Topics, see page 53. These topics can be used in place of the writing topic for this unit or as homework. The alternative topics relate to the theme of the unit but may not target the same grammar or rhetorical structures taught in the unit.

46   UNIT 2

CT A final writing task gives students an opportunity to integrate ideas, vocabulary, and grammar presented in the unit.

CT Students organize their ideas for writing using a particular structural or rhetorical pattern.

WRITE: A Complete Paragraph

WRITING A COMPLETE PARAGRAPH

A complete paragraph has **three parts**: a topic sentence, supporting sentences, and a conclusion. In this assignment, do the following in each part:

- **Topic sentence:** Introduce the topic and make a general statement. (This may be one or two sentences.)
- **Supporting sentences:** Explain the problem and the creative process you introduced in the topic sentence.
- **Conclusion:** Tell the end of the story, or make a final comment about the story.

1 Read the paragraph. Put brackets [ ] around the three parts of the paragraph.

Being curious helped me solve a big problem for my grandfather. He can't type emails or texts because he has very shaky hands. I was curious about iPads because so many people love them. I borrowed my friend's iPad and looked at all the games and other apps on the screen. I played a few games and learned about a few apps. But the best app was VoiceText. I touched it, I talked, then all of my words came on the screen. It was like someone else was typing my words! It made me think of my grandfather. He can't type, but he can talk! My cousins and I bought him an iPad with VoiceText, and now he can text or email us any time!

(continued on next page)

Creative Thinking   47

MyEnglishLab

Home | Help | Test student, reallylongname@emailaddress.com | Sign out

NORTHSTAR 2   READING & WRITING

1   Unit 1

Writing Skill: A Complete Paragraph

Read the paragraphs. Choose the answer that describes which part of the paragraph is missing.

I created a very original and delicious sandwich for myself last week. I wanted a peanut butter and jelly sandwich, but there was no jelly. I don't like peanut butter by itself. So I tried to find something else to put in the sandwich. I decided to combine lots of different foods with peanut butter. I made peanut butter sandwiches with cucumber, cheese, apple, chicken, potato, tomato, banana, ketchup, and mustard. Then I tasted each one.

1 ○ The topic sentence is missing.
  ○ The supporting sentences are missing.
  ○ The conclusion is missing.

I love growing tomatoes in my garden, but I am a terrible gardener. Most years, my tomatoes die because I forget to water them. One day I solved this gardening problem in my kitchen! Now my tomatoes get water for a whole day after I finish watering them. So if I forget for one or two days, they are fine.

ALWAYS LEARNING   PEARSON

MyEnglishLab

Key writing skills and strategies are reinforced and practiced in new contexts. Immediate feedback allows students and teachers to monitor progress and identify areas that need improvement.

Students continue through the writing process to learn revising techniques that help them move toward coherence and unity in their writing. Finally, students edit their work with the aid of a checklist that focuses on essential outcomes.

2 Each paragraph is missing one part. Circle the name of the part it is missing.

Paragraph 1

Last semester in English, I took a big risk and wrote a very creative essay about my grandmother. My teacher loved it and told me it was very creative. After that, I began to take more risks in my writing. Now I am a better writer, and I also enjoy it more.

What is missing?

a. Topic sentence

b. Supporting sentences

c. Conclusion

Paragraph 2

My history teacher last semester used a very creative way to teach our class. During the first class, she got angry with students because they looked at their phones during class. For the second class, she asked who had Twitter accounts. Half of the class raised their hands. She put us in pairs so that each pair had a phone with a Twitter account. She told us to search for the hashtag #hist232 in Twitter. We did, and we found a history question from her! We discussed the question with our partners, then tweeted the answer with the hashtag #hist232. We looked at all our answers on the big screen at the front of the class. We had interesting conversations with each other on Twitter and in person.

What is missing?

a. Topic sentence

b. Supporting sentences

c. Conclusion

3 Now go back to the first draft of your paragraph. What will your reader be curious to know more about? What can you add to give more information? Revise your paragraph and add something creative (like visuals) to help your reader understand your message.

GO TO MyEnglish**Lab** *FOR MORE SKILL PRACTICE.*

EDIT: Writing the Final Draft

Go to MyEnglishLab and write the final draft of your paragraph. Carefully edit it for grammatical and mechanical errors, such as spelling, capitalization, and punctuation. Make sure you use some of the vocabulary and grammar from the unit. Use the checklist to help you write your final draft. Then submit your paragraph to your teacher.

FINAL DRAFT CHECKLIST

❑ Does your paragraph tell about a time you or someone else used creative thinking?

❑ Does it have a topic sentence?

❑ Does it have supporting sentences that tell about the problem, and the creative thinking process?

❑ Does it have a conclusion that finishes the story or adds a comment to the story?

❑ Does it have a picture, chart, or other element that helps the reader understand the message better?

❑ Do you use past tense verbs correctly?

❑ Do you use new vocabulary that you learned in this unit?

3 Now write the first draft of your paragraph about a time you (or someone else) used creative thinking to solve a problem. Start with your topic sentence, explain the problem and the process, and then finish with a conclusion. Use the ideas in your chart on page 46 to help you write your paragraph.

REVISE: Using Your Creative Skills

Sometimes words do not communicate the whole message in a piece of writing. **Visuals** like pictures or charts can be useful, too. As you revise, use your creative skills, like including visuals, to communicate better with your readers. Combine writing with another skill that you have. Take a risk!

1 Read the revisions of the paragraphs and finish the sentence below each one.

Paragraph 1

Being curious helped me solve a big problem for my grandfather. He can't type emails or texts because he has very shaky hands. I was curious about iPads because so many people love them. I borrowed my friend's iPad and looked at all the games and other apps on the screen. I played a few games and learned about a few apps. But the best app was VoiceText. I touched it, I talked, then all of my words came on the screen. It was like someone else was typing my words! It made me think of my grandfather. He can't type, but he can talk! My cousins and I bought him an iPad with VoiceText, and now he can text or email us any time!

The picture gives the reader more information about _____.

INNOVATIVE TEACHING TOOLS

With instant access to a wide range of online content and diagnostic tools, teachers can customize learning environments to meet the needs of every student.

USING MyEnglishLab, NORTHSTAR TEACHERS CAN:

Deliver rich online content to engage and motivate students, including:

- student audio to support listening and speaking skills.
- engaging, authentic video clips, including reports adapted from ABC, NBC, and CBS newscasts, tied to the unit themes.
- opportunities for written and recorded reactions to be submitted by students.

Use a powerful selection of diagnostic reports to:

- view student scores by unit, skill, and activity.
- monitor student progress on any activity or test as often as needed.
- analyze class data to determine steps for remediation and support.

Use Teacher Resource eText* to access:

- a digital copy of the student book for whole-class instruction.
- downloadable achievement and placement tests.
- printable resources including lesson planners, videoscripts, and video activities.
- classroom audio.
- unit teaching notes and answer keys.

---

* Teacher Resource eText is accessible through MyEnglishLab: *NorthStar*.

COMPONENTS PRINT or eTEXT

STUDENT BOOK and MyEnglishLab

★ Student Book with MyEnglishLab

The two strands, Reading & Writing and Listening & Speaking, for each of the five levels, provide a fully blended approach with the seamless integration of print and online content. Students use MyEnglishLab to access additional practice online, view videos, listen to audio selections, and receive instant feedback on their work.

eTEXT and MyEnglishLab

★ eText with MyEnglishLab

Offering maximum flexibility for different learning styles and needs, a digital version of the student book can be used on iPad® and Android® devices.

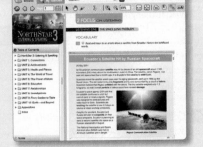

★ Instructor Access: Teacher Resource eText and MyEnglishLab (Reading & Writing 1–5)

Teacher Resource eText

Each level and strand of *NorthStar* has an accompanying Teacher Resource eText that includes: a digital student book, unit teaching notes, answer keys, downloadable achievement tests, classroom audio, lesson planners, video activities, videoscripts, and a downloadable placement test.

MyEnglishLab

Teachers assign MyEnglishLab activities to reinforce the skills students learn in class and monitor progress through an online gradebook. The automatically-graded exercises in MyEnglishLab *NorthStar* support and build on academic skills and vocabulary presented and practiced in the Student Book/eText. The teacher-graded activities include pronunciation, speaking, and writing, and are assigned by the instructor.

★ Classroom Audio CD

The Listening & Speaking audio contains the recordings and activities, as well as audio for the achievement tests. The Reading & Writing strand contains the readings on audio.

SCOPE AND SEQUENCE

UNIT OUTCOMES	1 WORK — FINDING THE IDEAL JOB — pages 2–25 — Reading 1: Finding the Ideal Job — Reading 2: The Ideal Job	2 STUDENT LIFE — CREATIVE THINKING — pages 26–53 — Reading 1: Can We Teach Creative Thinking in Schools? — Reading 2: Tips for Success in College: How to Be Creative
READING	• Make and confirm predictions • Identify the main ideas in a reading • Identify different types of supporting details • Scan a text to locate specific information • Predict content of a reading from visuals MyEnglishLab Vocabulary and Reading Skill Practice	• Make and confirm predictions • Identify the main ideas in a reading • Identify different types of supporting details • Scan a text to understand chronology • Recognize examples in a text MyEnglishLab Vocabulary and Reading Skill Practice
WRITING	• Organize ideas in a list • Identify the topic sentence of a paragraph • Support a main idea with details and examples • Edit and revise writing for content, language, and conventions **Task:** Write a paragraph with a topic sentence and supporting details and examples MyEnglishLab Writing Skill Practice and Writing Task	• Organize ideas in a chart • Add information to give extra support to the reader • Edit and revise writing for content, language, and conventions **Task:** Write a paragraph telling a story with a topic sentence, supporting details, and a conclusion MyEnglishLab Writing Skill Practice and Writing Task
INFERENCE	• Infer the author's opinion	• Infer connections between general statements and examples
VOCABULARY	• Infer word meaning from context MyEnglishLab Vocabulary Practice	• Infer word meaning from context MyEnglishLab Vocabulary Practice
GRAMMAR	• Distinguish between and use possessive and descriptive adjectives MyEnglishLab Grammar Practice	• Recognize and use past tense with regular/irregular past simple forms MyEnglishLab Grammar Practice
VIDEO	MyEnglishLab Interview with a Skydiving Instructor, Video Activity	MyEnglishLab College Students Spark Creativity in Kids, Voice of America, Video Activity
ASSESSMENTS	MyEnglishLab Check What You Know, Checkpoints 1 and 2, Unit 1 Achievement Test	MyEnglishLab Check What You Know, Checkpoints 1 and 2, Unit 2 Achievement Test

3 MONEY
MAKING MONEY
pages 54–79

Reading 1: Making Money
Reading 2: I Made It Myself

4 ETIQUETTE
SUBWAY ETIQUETTE
pages 80–105

Reading 1: A Civilized Suggestion
Reading 2: Riding the Subway in Japan

• Make and confirm predictions • Identify the main ideas in a reading • Identify different types of supporting details • Scan a text to locate specific information • Follow chronological sequence • Compare information from two readings MyEnglishLab Vocabulary and Reading Skill Practice	• Make and confirm predictions • Identify the main ideas in a reading • Identify different types of supporting details • Scan a text to locate specific information • Identify the main elements of a story (background information, conflict, climax, and resolution) • Compare and contrast information from two readings MyEnglishLab Vocabulary and Reading Skill Practice
• Write sentences of comparison • Organize ideas using a cluster diagram • Edit and revise writing for content, language, and conventions **Task:** Write a well-organized paragraph with clear explanations MyEnglishLab Writing Skill Practice and Writing Task	• Write responses to letters • Organize ideas in a list • Create sentences using parallel structure • Edit and redraft writing for content, language, and conventions **Task:** Write an informational Web page MyEnglishLab Writing Skill Practice and Writing Task
• Infer information about situations in the future	• Infer the author's attitude
• Infer word meaning from context • Recognize antonyms MyEnglishLab Vocabulary Practice	• Infer word meaning from context • Recognize word forms (nouns, verbs, adjectives) MyEnglishLab Vocabulary Practice
• Recognize and use the comparative form of adjectives MyEnglishLab Grammar Practice	• Recognize and use imperatives to give instructions and make polite requests MyEnglishLab Grammar Practice
MyEnglishLab *The History of Money*, Video Activity	MyEnglishLab *How to Ask for a Date*, Video Activity
MyEnglishLab Check What You Know, Checkpoints 1 and 2, Unit 3 Achievement Test	MyEnglishLab Check What You Know, Checkpoints 1 and 2, Unit 4 Achievement Test

SCOPE AND SEQUENCE

UNIT OUTCOMES	5 FOOD **WE ARE WHAT WE EAT** pages 106–131 *Reading 1: A New Fish in Town* *Reading 2: Making Sense of the American Diet*	6 HEROES **THE HEART OF A HERO** pages 132–157 *Reading 1: What is a Hero?* *Reading 2: Book Review: Harry Potter and the Sorcerer's Stone*
READING	• Make and confirm predictions • Identify the main ideas in each paragraph of a reading • Identify different types of supporting details • Scan a text to locate specific information • Analyze advantages and disadvantages MyEnglishLab Vocabulary and Reading Skill Practice	• Make and confirm predictions • Identify the main ideas in a reading • Identify different types of supporting details • Scan a text to locate specific information • Follow chronological sequence in a reading MyEnglishLab Vocabulary and Reading Skill Practice
WRITING	• Organize ideas using an e-chart • Support main ideas with reasons • Express contrasting ideas using but and however • Edit and revise writing for content, language, and conventions **Task:** Write a well-organized paragraph MyEnglishLab Writing Skill Practice and Writing Task	• Organize ideas using a list and an outline • Add examples and explanations to give extra support to the reader • Edit and revise writing for content, language, and conventions **Task:** Write a paragraph telling a story MyEnglishLab Writing Skill Practice and Writing Task
INFERENCE	• Infer facts	• Infer meaning from metaphors
VOCABULARY	• Infer word meaning from context • Recognize and use word forms (nouns, verbs, adjectives, adverbs) MyEnglishLab Vocabulary Practice	• Infer word meaning from context • Recognize and use word forms (nouns, verbs, adjectives, adverbs) MyEnglishLab Vocabulary Practice
GRAMMAR	• Recognize and use too much/too many/too + adjective MyEnglishLab Grammar Practice	• Recognize and use time clauses in the present tense MyEnglishLab Grammar Practice
VIDEO	MyEnglishLab *Food from the Hood*, Video Activity	MyEnglishLab *All for One*, ABC News, Video Activity
ASSESSMENTS	MyEnglishLab Check What You Know, Checkpoints I and 2, Unit 5 Achievement Test	MyEnglishLab Check What You Know, Checkpoints I and 2, Unit 6 Achievement Test

7 HEALTH
WHAT'S YOUR MEDICINE?
pages 158–185
Reading 1: Leech
Reading 2: Gross Medicine

8 ENDANGERED CULTURES
ENDANGERED CULTURES
pages 186–215
Reading 1: Will Indigenous Cultures Survive?
Reading 2: The Penan

• Use a title and headings to predict content • Identify the main ideas in a reading • Identify different types of supporting details • Scan a text to locate specific information • Take double entry notes to interact with the text MyEnglishLab Vocabulary and Reading Skill Practice	• Study a map • Use a title to predict content • Identify the main ideas in a reading • Identify different types of supporting details and examples • Scan a text to locate specific information • Understand the purpose of quoted speech in a text • Support general statements in one text with examples from another text MyEnglishLab Vocabulary and Reading Skill Practice
• Organize ideas using a cluster diagram • Signal basic chronological sequence using time order words • Edit and revise writing for content, language, and conventions **Task:** Write a personal narrative paragraph MyEnglishLab Writing Skill Practice and Writing Task	• Organize ideas using an outline • Take notes from a reading to support an opinion • Support a main idea with reasons • Recognize and write concluding sentences • Edit and revise writing for content, language, and conventions **Task:** Write a paragraph that makes a prediction MyEnglishLab Writing Skill Practice and Writing Task
• Use inferences to make judgments about information in a text	• Infer the author's attitude
• Infer word meaning from context MyEnglishLab Vocabulary Practice	• Infer word meaning from context MyEnglishLab Vocabulary Practice
• Recognize and use a variety of adverbs of manner MyEnglishLab Grammar Practice	• Recognize and use *be going to* to make predictions • Recognize and use *will* to make predictions • Recognize and use the present progressive to describe future events MyEnglishLab Grammar Practice
MyEnglishLab *Chinese Medicine*, Video Activity	MyEnglishLab *Maori Cultures*, Video Activity
MyEnglishLab Check What You Know, Checkpoints 1 and 2, Unit 7 Achievement Test	MyEnglishLab Check What You Know, Checkpoints 1 and 2, Unit 8 Achievement Test

REVIEWERS

Chris Antonellis, Boston University – CELOP; Gail August, Hostos; Aegina Barnes, York College; Kim Bayer, Hunter College; Mine Bellikli, Atilim University; Allison Blechman, Embassy CES; Paul Blomquist, Kaplan; Helena Botros, FLS; James Branchick, FLS; Chris Bruffee, Embassy CES; Nese Cakli, Duzce University; María Cordani Tourinho Dantas, Colégio Rainha De Paz; Jason Davis, ASC English; Lindsay Donigan, Fullerton College; Bina Dugan, BCCC; Sibel Ece Izmir, Atilim University; Érica Ferrer, Universidad del Norte; María Irma Gallegos Peláez, Universidad del Valle de México; Jeff Gano, ASA College; María Genovev a Chávez Bazán, Universidad del Valle de México; Juan Garcia, FLS; Heidi Gramlich, The New England School of English; Phillip Grayson, Kaplan; Rebecca Gross, The New England School of English; Rick Guadiana, FLS; Sebnem Guzel, Tobb University; Esra Hatipoglu, Ufuk University; Brian Henry, FLS; Josephine Horna, BCCC; Arthur Hui, Fullerton College; Zoe Isaacson, Hunter College; Kathy Johnson, Fullerton College; Marcelo Juica, Urban College of Boston; Tom Justice, North Shore Community College; Lisa Karakas, Berkeley College; Eva Kopernacki, Embassy CES; Drew Larimore, Kaplan; Heidi Lieb, BCCC; Patricia Martins, Ibeu; Cecilia Mora Espejo, Universidad del Valle de México; Kate Nyhan, The New England School of English; Julie Oni, FLS; Willard Osman, The New England School of English; Olga Pagieva, ASA College; Manish Patel, FLS; Paige Poole, Universidad del Norte; Claudia Rebello, Ibeu; Lourdes Rey, Universidad del Norte; Michelle Reynolds, FLS International Boston Commons; Mary Ritter, NYU; Minerva Santos, Hostos; Sezer Sarioz, Saint Benoit PLS; Ebru Sinar, Tobb University; Beth Soll, NYU (Columbia); Christopher Stobart, Universidad del Norte; Guliz Uludag, Ufuk University; Debra Un, NYU; Hilal Unlusu, Saint Benoit PLS; María del Carmen Viruega Trejo, Universidad del Valle de México; Reda Vural, Atilim University; Douglas Waters, Universidad del Norte; Leyla Yucklik, Duzce University; Jorge Zepeda Porras, Universidad del Valle de México

FINDING THE
Ideal Job

1. What job or profession does this person have?

2. Would you like to do this job? Explain your answer.

3. What is the ideal job for you?

GO TO MyEnglishLab TO CHECK WHAT YOU KNOW.

2 FOCUS ON READING

READING ONE | FINDING THE IDEAL JOB

VOCABULARY

Read the list of words and their definitions.

advice: an opinion you give someone about what he or she should do	**managers:** people who direct and organize groups of workers in a company
careers: the kinds of work people do, usually after learning how and usually for a long time	**postings:** ads or comments on the Internet
	résumés: written descriptions of people's education and previous jobs
hire: to give someone a job	**rewards:** good things you get in return for work (such as money or health insurance)
ideal: perfect	
interviews: meetings where a person looking for a job talks to the person who is looking for a new worker	**skills:** things that you can do well; abilities that you have learned and practiced
	setting: the place where something happens

Now use the words from the list to complete this news article about American workers and companies.

What Today's Worker Wants

In 2012, 7.8 percent of Americans were out of work. And many of the people who had jobs

were also looking for new ones because they weren't happy with their current jobs.

According to a 2012 survey, less than half of all American workers really love their jobs. Most

of these workers want to change their jobs. This is a problem for workers, and it is also a problem

for companies. Thirty-three percent of _____managers_____ say that they don't care what
                                        1.

happens to their companies—and those are the people who are supposed to be in charge![1]

What do workers want? Usually we think that everyone wants more money, but today's

workers are looking for other _____. They want health insurance and more
                                2.

vacation. They also want to know that they will learn new _____ at a job. Older
                                                            3.

---

[1] **be in charge:** be responsible for a group of people or an activity

workers are usually happier with their jobs than younger workers. This is probably because they

have had time to think about their _____ and find a job they like.
                                                 4.

Many companies today try to make changes to keep workers happy. They ask their workers

questions about what makes them really happy at work. Many technology companies create

comfortable _____ for their workers: they have health clubs, fancy coffee
                         5.

machines, and soft sofas for relaxing. If a worker likes to be at his job, he will work harder and

stay at the company.

If workers leave, companies have to _____ new people. And that takes a lot of
                                                      6.

time. They have to write _____ to put on the Internet. They have to read hundreds
                                     7.

of _____. They have to do _____ to meet people who want to
          8.   9.

work there. And even after all that work, they might not find the _____ new
                                                                              10.

worker.

Our _____ to new college graduates: Take your time and choose carefully.
          11.

■■■■■■■■■■■■■■■■■■■■■■■■■■■■■■■■■■ GO TO MyEnglishLab FOR MORE VOCABULARY PRACTICE.

PREVIEW

Imagine you are not satisfied with your job. You decide to job hunt—that is, to look for a new job. With a partner, write a list of things you might do to find a job.

1. *I might ask someone in my family for a job.* _____

2. _____

3. _____

4. _____

Now learn what a professional has to say about this topic. Read a book review of a job-hunting manual.

FINDING THE IDEAL JOB

What Color Is Your Parachute?

A Practical Manual for Job-Hunters and Career Changers, 2014 Edition

by Richard N. Bolles, Ten Speed Press, $18.99.

1 You are out of work. You hate your job. You aren't satisfied with your **career**. You are looking for your first job. Where do you start?

2 If you are like most Americans, you'll probably email your **résumé** to a lot of companies. You might search for job **postings** on the Internet or spend hours and hours working on your LinkedIn[1] page. But experts[2] say you won't have much luck. People find jobs only 5 to 10 percent of the time when they look for jobs in these ways. So what can you do?

3 One thing you can do is read Richard Bolles's *What Color Is Your Parachute?*[3] Bolles is an expert in job hunting. He has helped thousands of people find jobs and careers. This book is different from other job-hunting manuals. Bolles doesn't help you to find just another job. Instead, he helps you find your **ideal** job: a job that fits you, a job that makes you happy. What kind of job is ideal for you? If you don't know the answer, Bolles says, you can't find your ideal job. You need to have a clear picture in your mind of the job you want. The book has many exercises to help you draw this picture.

4 Bolles says that you must think about three things before you can find your ideal job:

(1) **YOUR SKILLS.** What do you like to do? What do you do well? Are you good at talking to groups? Growing vegetables? Teaching? Drawing on the computer? Bolles asks you to think about all your **skills**, not only "work skills." For example, a mother of four children is probably good at managing people (children!). This woman may be a good **manager**.

(2) **JOB SETTING.** Where do you like to work? Do you like to work outside? At home? In an office? Alone or with others? What kinds of people do you like to work with?

(3) **JOB REWARDS.** How much money do you need? How much money do you want? Do you need a lot of vacation time? What else do you want from a job? What makes you feel good about a job?

5 After Bolles helps you decide on your ideal job, he gives you specific **advice** on how to find that job. One of his favorite tools for finding a job is networking. Networking

---

[1] **LinkedIn:** an online professional networking site

[2] **experts:** people who know a lot about something

[3] **parachute:** something you wear when you jump out of a plane. When you jump, it opens up, and it stops you from hitting the ground very hard.

means using every person you know either to give you information about a company or career or to introduce you to someone else who can give you this information. Bolles asks everyone he meets how they got their job. Nine times out of 10, they got their job because a friend knew someone at the company who hired them. So, once you know the kind of job you want, Bolles says you must use your network—everyone you know—to help you meet the one person who will help you get the job.

6 Bolles's chapter on job **interviews** is full of useful information and suggestions. For example, most people go to interviews asking themselves the question, "How do I get the company to **hire** me?" Bolles thinks this is the wrong question. Instead, he wants you to ask yourself, "Do I want to work here or not?"

7 Some people think that Bolles writes far too much and repeats himself. True, his book could be 100 pages instead of 364. But his writing style makes the book very easy to read, and a reader doesn't have to read the parts that seem less important. Other readers say that there is not enough space to write the answers to the exercises. But these are very small problems. *What Color Is Your Parachute?* is the best job-hunting manual you can buy.

8 *What Color Is Your Parachute?* was first written in 1970. Over 10 million copies have been sold since then. The information is updated[4] every year. So, if you are looking for a job or if you have a job but want a new one, remember: Don't just email your résumé out to every company. Don't just answer Internet job postings. And don't wait for friends to give you a job. Instead, buy this book and do a job hunt the right way.

---

[4] **updated:** changed to show new information

MAIN IDEAS

1 Look again at the Preview on page 5. How did your answers help you understand the book review?

2 Read each statement. Decide if it is true or false. Write **T** (true) or **F** (false) next to it. Compare your answers with a partner's.

_____ 1. *What Color Is Your Parachute?* is similar to other job-hunting manuals.

_____ 2. Bolles wants to help people find jobs on the Internet more quickly.

_____ 3. According to *What Color Is Your Parachute?*, job hunters should think about their skills, the job setting, and the job rewards they want.

_____ 4. *What Color Is Your Parachute?* includes specific advice on finding jobs.

_____ 5. The reviews of Bolles's book are all positive.

DETAILS

Look at the list of job-hunting methods. Decide where each one should go in the chart. Write each method in the correct column.

- decide what kind of job is ideal
- decide what kind of place you want to work in
- do exercises in *What Color Is Your Parachute?*
- ~~look on the Internet~~
- update your LinkedIn page
- send out lots of résumés
- think about job rewards
- think about your skills

FIND A JOB	
WHAT MANY PEOPLE DO	WHAT BOLLES SAYS WILL HELP YOU
look on the Internet	

MAKE INFERENCES

INFERRING THE AUTHOR'S OPINION

An **inference** is an educated guess about something that is not stated directly in a text. Sometimes careful readers can understand an author's opinion (ideas or beliefs about a particular subject) even when it is not stated directly. They can **infer** this opinion.

Look at the example and read the explanation.

- Kleppinger believes that Bolles's book is hard because it's so long.   TRUE   FALSE

    (Answer: FALSE)

In paragraph 7, the author says that *some* people think Bolles writes too much and repeats himself. At this point, we don't know her opinion. But then she says that his book is easy to read.

After reading the text closely, we can infer the author's opinion: She doesn't think Bolles's book is hard just because it's long.

Read each statement about what Kleppinger believes about Richard Bolles's book. Decide if it is *True* or *False*. Check (✓) the appropriate box.

KLEPPINGER BELIEVES . . .	PARAGRAPH	TRUE	FALSE
1. It's fun to read Bolles's book.	3,7		
2. Bolles's exercises are too hard.	3,7		
3. Anyone looking for a job should read Bolles's book.	8		

EXPRESS OPINIONS

Discuss the questions with a partner. Give your opinions. Then share your answers with the class.

1. The next time you look for a job, which of Bolles's ideas do you think you might use?

2. You are in an interview for a job with a very interesting company. Based on Bolles's advice, what questions might you ask the interviewer about this company?

3. The title of the book is *What Color Is Your Parachute?* Why do you think the author chose this title?

■■■■■■■■■■■■■■■■■■■■■■ *GO TO* MyEnglishLab *TO GIVE YOUR OPINION ABOUT ANOTHER QUESTION.*

READ

1 Look at the boldfaced words in the reading and think about the questions.

    1. Which words do you know the meaning of?

    2. Can you use any of the words in a sentence?

2 JOBMOB is a blog that posts about interesting and unusual jobs. Read about some people who have found their ideal job in some very unexpected places.

JOB MOB

THE IDEAL JOB
By Alex Frost

HOME

CONTACT

ABOUT US

1   Believe it or not, some people get paid for doing the things that make them really happy. Read about a few people who have the jobs of their dreams.

"I get paid to make videos!"

2   When I was 14, my uncle gave me his old video camera, and I started making videos. I didn't do very well in school, but I loved getting to know people and making videos about them. I taught myself to edit the videos on a simple computer program of my dad's. One day a friend of my mom's asked me to make a video of her family. She wanted to send it to her mother who lived in China. It was a lot of fun, and she paid me $150. Soon her friends asked me to make videos for them, and suddenly I had a business. That was 10 years ago. Things change a lot in this work, so I'm always taking classes. But I have to say I love **running my own business**.

"I have the greatest job in the world."

3   These days almost everyone turns to the Internet when they are single and want to meet someone. There are many Internet dating sites. But most people don't know how important it is to have a personal touch. What do I do? I am a matchmaker with 41 years of **experience**. Because of me, 60 couples are now happily married or engaged. I have a very good eye for people. And I don't mean  I match people on how they look. I mean, I can meet a person just once for 10 minutes, and I know for sure what kind of person he or she is. I get a feeling. And this feeling tells me, "Oh, he might be a great husband for Stephanie," or "Ah, now here is the woman for Timothy." I can't imagine a job that's more fun. I meet wonderful people. I work for myself. Nobody tells me what to do. I don't spend much time with a computer in an office—the whole city is my office! I make enough money to live a simple life. And I get so much joy from seeing what happens to my matches. A month ago, a couple stopped by on their way home from the hospital with their new baby girl. I'm so happy to think that I helped make that family!

"I have a job with an incredible view."

4   Teaching skydiving[1] is exciting. I get to be outside, and I love seeing students on their first jump. They are nervous and excited. For them, that first step out of the plane is the biggest **challenge**. After they take that step, it's all good. When they get to the ground, they can't wait to call everyone they know and tell them they just jumped out of an airplane. Later,  when they learn to turn and fly forward, they realize that they're not just flying stones. They realize that they're like birds—they can fly!

5   It wasn't easy to get this job. I had to have about 1,000 jumps and about two years of **training**. And the **salary** was only $15,000 for the first year. But I don't do it for the money. In fact, I don't need to get paid at all. I love it that much!

---

[1] **skydiving:** the sport of jumping out of airplanes with a parachute

COMPREHENSION

Complete the sentences with the correct name from the reading.

1. _____Don_____ made $15,000 his first year.

2. _____ helped 60 couples find each other.

3. _____ didn't do well in school as a child.

4. _____ has the same job she had over 40 years ago.

5. _____ is studying to get better skills.

6. _____ loves teaching.

7. _____ studied and practiced for his job for two years.

8. _____ is in charge of a video business.

■■ GO TO MyEnglishLab FOR MORE VOCABULARY PRACTICE.

READING SKILL

1 Look at the photos in Reading Two. Do the photos help you understand the reading?

PREDICTING CONTENT FROM VISUALS

Before reading any text, strong readers look at all the **visuals** (pictures, photos, graphs, etc.) on the page. This gets them to think about what they already know about the topic and allows them to **predict the content of** the text.

For example:

In the photo for paragraph 2, I see a man behind a video camera.

The paragraph must be about a man whose ideal job is to make videos.

2 Work with a partner. Discuss the questions about the photographs in Reading Two.

1. Look closely at the photo for paragraph 3.

   What do you see in the photo that helped you better understand paragraph 3?

2. Look closely at the photo for paragraphs 4 and 5.

   What do you see in the photo that helped you better understand paragraphs 4 and 5?

■■ GO TO MyEnglishLab FOR MORE SKILL PRACTICE.

STEP 1: Organize

Look at Reading One (**R1**) again. Reread paragraph 4 about skills, setting, and rewards. Then look at this list of ideas from Reading Two (**R2**) and decide where each one should go in the chart. Write each idea in the correct column.

- ~~editing video~~
- making $15,000/year
- working outside
- seeing people learn
- skydiving
- teaching
- understanding how people get along
- working in an office
- running a business
- working on a computer
- seeing happy couples I introduced
- working with people

SKILLS	SETTINGS	REWARDS
editing video		

STEP 2: Synthesize

How could the people in Reading Two answer the interview questions? Choose one of them (circle his/her name) and write the answers for that person. Use information from the chart in Step 1.

1. Q: (Ryan)/Amanda/Don, what are your skills?

   A: _I have some video-editing skills._

2. Q: Ryan/Amanda/Don, what are your skills?

   A: _____

   _____

3. Q: What kind of setting do you like working in?

   A: _____

   _____

4. Q: What rewards are important to you?

   A: _____

   _____

GO TO MyEnglishLab TO CHECK WHAT YOU LEARNED.

3 FOCUS ON WRITING

VOCABULARY

REVIEW

Put the three sentences in each group in order. Write *1, 2,* or *3* next to each sentence.

a. __1__ I saw a **posting** for an interesting job.

  __3__ The company called and asked me to come in for an **interview**.

  __2__ I sent my **résumé** to the company.

b. _____ Mr. Fredericks went to school for more **training**.

  _____ Mr. Fredericks wanted to change **careers**.

  _____ Mr. Fredericks realized he needed new **skills** to find another job.

c. _____ Myron realized that he needed to pay a higher **salary** because no one was interested.

  _____ Myron put **postings** on the Internet for a new manager.

  _____ Myron's best **manager** quit.

d. _____ John was looking for someone with strong **skills** in photographing food.

  _____ John **hired** Karen.

  _____ John met Karen, who is **ideal** because she made ads for restaurants.

e. _____ Kelly quit because she wanted a job with different **rewards**.

  _____ Kelly is **running her own business**.

  _____ Kelly had a big **salary** at her last job, but she did not like the job.

f. _____ Theo had 20 years of **experience** as a cook.

  _____ Theo decided to find a new **career**.

  _____ Cooking was no longer a **challenge** for Theo.

g. _____ Her brother told Lily Rose to find a job with a great **setting**.

  _____ Her brother thought about the **rewards** Lily Rose might want from a job.

  _____ Lily Rose asked her brother for **advice** on job hunting.

EXPAND

Each word or phrase in parentheses changes the meaning of the sentence. Cross out the word or phrase that does not make sense.

1. Kate's salary is (huge / pretty good / ~~expensive~~).

2. The rewards at my last job were (happy / great / not very good).

3. You will get some (teaching / technical / lazy) skills at this job.

4. Vladimir is a very (organized / long / unfriendly) manager.

5. Julie's friend gave her (useful / bad / used) advice.

6. I want to move up in my job, so I'm signing up for some more (setting / advanced / regular) training.

7. Sam works in a(n) (outdoor / delicious / beautiful) setting.

8. I want to work with (manager / smart / friendly) people.

9. For this job, you must have plenty of (experience / advice / skills).

10. Some workers really enjoy working (alone / on teams / in settings).

CREATE

Complete the email this college student is writing to his parents about his job search. Use the words from the box for items 1–3. For items 4–6, complete the sentences in your own words using new words from the unit.

advice	résumé	skills

Dear Mom and Dad,

Stop worrying. I've got this job thing all worked out. I have a degree in Computer Science. Any

company will see that my computer _____ are excellent. My professor at school
1.

has given me a lot of good _____ about how to get a job next year.
2.

First, she says I should make sure my _____ is on my LinkedIn page.
3.

Second, she wants me to _____.
4.

Third, she thinks I should _____.
5.

Fourth, she wants me to _____.
6.

So don't worry. You see I have it all under control.

Love,

Nick

■■■■■■■■■■■■■■■■■■■■■■■■■■■■■■■■■■■■■■ GO TO MyEnglishLab FOR MORE VOCABULARY PRACTICE.

GRAMMAR

1 Read the email. Notice the boldfaced words. They are two kinds of adjectives: **descriptive adjectives** and **possessive adjectives**.

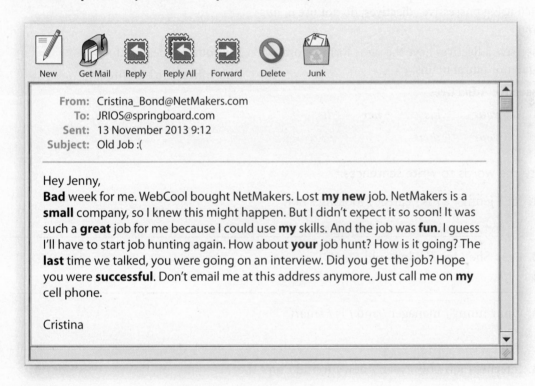

New   Get Mail   Reply   Reply All   Forward   Delete   Junk

From: Cristina_Bond@NetMakers.com
To: JRIOS@springboard.com
Sent: 13 November 2013 9:12
Subject: Old Job :(

Hey Jenny,
Bad week for me. WebCool bought NetMakers. Lost **my new** job. NetMakers is a **small** company, so I knew this might happen. But I didn't expect it so soon! It was such a **great** job for me because I could use **my** skills. And the job was **fun**. I guess I'll have to start job hunting again. How about **your** job hunt? How is it going? The **last** time we talked, you were going on an interview. Did you get the job? Hope you were **successful**. Don't email me at this address anymore. Just call me on **my** cell phone.

Cristina

List each adjective in the email on one of the lines.

1. Descriptive adjectives _bad,_____

2. Possessive adjectives _my,_____

Finding the Ideal Job 17

DESCRIPTIVE AND POSSESSIVE ADJECTIVES

1. Descriptive adjectives describe nouns.	The teacher **is** *funny.*
They can come after the verb *be.*	
They can come before a noun.	She is a *funny* teacher.
When a noun follows an adjective, use *a, an,* or *the* before the adjective. (*A* and *an* are used only with count nouns.)	She's **a** *funny* **teacher.**
	She's **an** *important* **writer.**
	The *new* **teacher** isn't here.
REMEMBER: Do not use *a, an,* or *the* when the adjective is not followed by a noun.	Gary is *smart.*
2. Possessive adjectives show belonging.	I have a job. *My* **job** is very interesting.
A noun always follows a possessive adjective. When using possessive adjectives, do not use *a, an,* or *the.*	*His* **boss** is nice.
Possessive adjectives have the same form before singular or plural nouns.	*Your* **office** is beautiful.
	Your **offices** are beautiful.

Possessive Adjectives

my	*your*	*his*	*her*	*its*
our	*your*	*their*		

2 Use the words to write sentences.

1. for / Jenny / a / is / career / looking / new

Jenny is looking for a new career.

2. like / She / job / didn't / old / her

_____

3. Our / funny / manager / and / is / smart

_____

4. Internet / job / his / Juan / new / found / on / the

_____

5. sister / out / work / of / is / My

_____

6. an / Richard Bolles / job / interesting / has

_____

7. wife / has / office / David's / a / huge

_____

8. Tom / Andrea / business / and / their / sold

_____

9. pays / That / well / company / workers / very / its

_____

10. résumé / has / a / Dee / great

_____

3 Describe the pictures. For each picture, write at least three sentences. Use at least one possessive adjective, one descriptive adjective before a noun, and one descriptive adjective after **be**. You can use the descriptive adjectives from the box.

big	dirty	hungry	messy	sad	sleepy	young
curly	happy	long	old	short	straight	

1. The man:

The man is young. He has short hair. He is hungry.

He drives an old truck.

The truck:

His truck is old. The old truck is dirty.

2. The woman:

_____

_____

The desk:

_____

3. The doctor:

_____

_____

The patient:

_____

_____

■■■■■■■■■■ *GO TO* MyEnglishLab *FOR MORE GRAMMAR PRACTICE AND TO CHECK WHAT YOU LEARNED.*

FINAL WRITING TASK

In this unit, you read about how to find your ideal job and about people who found their ideal job. Think about *your* ideal job. Why is that job ideal for you?

You are going to **write a paragraph about your ideal job.** You will explain why this job is ideal for you. You will tell about the skills, setting, and rewards related to this job. Use the vocabulary and grammar from the unit.*

PREPARE TO WRITE: Listing

In order to help you think about the topic for your paragraph, you will do a prewriting activity called **listing**. Listing is making a list of your ideas before you begin to write. When you make a list, it is not necessary to write complete sentences *(see the lists on pages 8 and 13)*.

1 Richard Bolles says that you need to know your skills, preferred settings, and rewards in order to find your ideal job. List these things in the chart. Then list some possible ideal jobs for you.

SKILLS I HAVE	SETTINGS I PREFER	REWARDS I WANT

Possible Ideal Jobs for Me

_____

_____

_____

---

* For Alternative Writing Topics, see page 25. These topics can be used in place of the writing topic for this unit or as homework. The alternative topics relate to the theme of the unit but may not target the same grammar or rhetorical structures taught in the unit.

2 Find a classmate who knows you well. Show your list to this classmate. See if he or she has any more ideas about jobs that might be good for you and add them to the list. Then choose an ideal job to write about.

WRITE: A Paragraph and Its Topic Sentence

A **paragraph** is a group of sentences about one topic. The first sentence is the **topic sentence**. It states the main idea of the paragraph. For this assignment, the topic sentence will give the name of the writer's ideal job.

1 Read the paragraph. Then underline the topic sentence and circle the name of the writer's ideal job.

> I want to be a mountain climbing guide. I like this job for several reasons. First of all, mountain climbing is very exciting. Mountain climbing guides get to climb tall, dangerous mountains. Second, I enjoy working outside. I like the fresh air much better than I like a stuffy office. Finally, I like to meet interesting people. Mountain climbing guides travel to many different parts of the world and meet other adventurous people.

2 Each paragraph is missing a topic sentence. Choose the best one below and write it on the line. Remember that the topic sentence must give the name of the writer's ideal job.

Paragraph 1

_____.

There are many reasons why I like this job. First, I like animals. Animals bring a lot of joy to our lives, but they do not ask for a lot in return. I also enjoy helping animals and their owners feel better. Pet owners are happy when their pets are well. Finally, veterinarians get to work with other people who like animals. They can even bring their pets to work!

Topic Sentences

    a. I would like a job working with animals.

    b. I think I would like to become a veterinarian.

    c. A veterinarian helps people and animals feel better.

(continued on next page)

Paragraph 2

_____.

Many people think accountants have boring jobs, but I think accounting is interesting. I like math, and I am good at it. I also like helping people manage their money. So I think I have the skills to be an accountant. Accountants mostly work alone. I like meeting people, but I prefer to work alone. Good accountants can earn a lot of money, and that is important for me.

Topic Sentences

  a. Accountants are very important for businesses and people.

  b. I would like to be a mathematician.

  c. My ideal job is to be an accountant.

3 Write the topic sentence for the paragraph that you are going to write about your ideal job.

Your topic sentence: _____

4 Now write the first draft of your paragraph about your ideal job. Start with your topic sentence. Then write sentences that explain the idea in your topic sentence. Use the list you made on page 20 to help you write your paragraph.

REVISE: Adding Supporting Sentences

Sentences that come after the topic sentence are **supporting sentences**. They explain the main idea with specific details and examples.

1 Read the paragraph. Underline the topic sentence. Then discuss with a partner what kind of information the writer could add to the paragraph.

I would like to become a computer animator and make films like _Brave, The Avengers,_ and _The Hobbit_. This job is ideal for me because I love to work on computers, and I love to draw.

It is important for me to work with fun people, and everyone I know in animation is really fun.

Animators can make a lot of money, and that is important.

2 Read each paragraph and list of supporting sentences. Choose **two** sentences to add to the paragraph. Use an arrow to show where each sentence should go. Put the sentences about skills together, the sentences about setting together, and the sentences about rewards together.

Paragraph 1

I would like to become a computer animator and make films like *Brave, The Avengers,* and *The Hobbit.* This job is ideal for me because I love to work on computers, and I love to draw. It is important for me to work with fun people, and everyone I know in animation is really fun. Animators can make a lot of money, and that is important.

Supporting Sentences

a. I always buy a large popcorn when I go to the movies.

b. But the best reward is that I get to see films I helped to make in theaters.

c. I also know how to draw Manga animations.

d. Mickey Mouse was one of Walt Disney's first animations.

Paragraph 2

Fashion designing is my dream job. I have good skills for designing clothes. Fashion designers have a lot of fun in their jobs. They can work alone at home or in a studio with others. One reward is that they get to see people wearing their designs. Designing clothes sounds like a lot of fun!

Supporting Sentences

a. I love wearing Dolce and Gabbana clothes.

b. I know how to sew, and I love to draw clothes.

c. Designing shoes could also be a fun job because I like shoes.

d. Fashion designers also get to travel, and I love to travel.

3 Now go back to the first draft of your paragraph. Do all your sentences support the topic sentence? If not, cross them out. Then add some more supporting sentences. Make sure these sentences explain the topic sentence with details and examples.

GO TO MyEnglishLab *FOR MORE SKILL PRACTICE.*

EDIT: Writing the Final Draft

Go to MyEnglishLab and write the final draft of your paragraph. Carefully edit it for grammatical and mechanical errors such as spelling, capitalization, and punctuation. Make sure you use some of the vocabulary and grammar from the unit. Use the checklist to help you write your final draft. Then submit your paragraph to your teacher.

FINAL DRAFT CHECKLIST

- ❑ Does your paragraph tell about your ideal job?

- ❑ Does it tell about the skills, setting, and rewards related to this job?

- ❑ Does it contain a topic sentence?

- ❑ Are there enough supporting sentences to explain the topic sentence?

- ❑ Do the supporting sentences give reasons why the job is ideal for you?

- ❑ Do you use descriptive adjectives and possessive adjectives correctly?

- ❑ Do you use new vocabulary that you learned in this unit?

UNIT PROJECT

Work in pairs. Interview someone who wants to change careers. This person might be a classmate, a teacher, a neighbor, or a relative. Follow these steps:

STEP 1: With your partner, prepare a list of questions for your interview. You could start with the following questions and then add some questions of your own to the list.

- What is your name?

- What is your career now?

- What do you do?

- What are the good and bad things about your career?

- What is your ideal career? Why?

- Why would you like this career better than the one you have now?

- _____

- _____

STEP 2: Interview the person with your partner. One of you asks the questions, and the other one takes notes.

STEP 3: After the interview, research online the job the person is leaving and the job he or she is going to.

STEP 4: You and your partner write a paragraph. Describe the job that person has and the job that he or she wants. Explain why he or she dreams about a different kind of career. Use any ideas you learned from the readings to help you write.

STEP 5: Share your writing with another pair. Read the other pair's paragraph.

ALTERNATIVE WRITING TOPICS

Write about one of the topics below. Use the vocabulary and grammar from the unit.

1. Imagine your friend just finished college and doesn't know what to do for work. Write him or her an email with advice. Use information from the review of *What Color Is Your Parachute?* Give at least three suggestions.

2. Do you know anyone who has his or her dream job? Write a paragraph about this person. Answer these questions:
   - Who is he or she?
   - What does he or she do?
   - How did he or she get the job?
   - What is most important to him or her about the job?

GO TO MyEnglishLab TO WRITE ABOUT ONE OF THE ALTERNATIVE TOPICS, WATCH A VIDEO ABOUT AN OFFBEAT JOB, AND TAKE THE UNIT 1 ACHIEVEMENT TEST.

CREATIVE
Thinking

1. What are the students learning in this class?

2. How will the teacher decide their grades?

3. What is the difference between this class and other classes like Math or English?

GO TO MyEnglishLab TO CHECK WHAT YOU KNOW.

VOCABULARY

1 Read the list of sample test questions and the list of academic subjects. Match each question with the appropriate subject. Pay attention to the boldfaced words.

Sample Test Questions

_____ 1. **Create** a 3D model of an Egyptian pyramid.

_____ 2. Write a one-page essay about the 1920s in the United States. **Focus on** one of the following areas in your essay: government, fashion, technology.

_____ 3. Is the following a **fact** or an opinion? World War II ended in 1945.

_____ 4. If x=7 and y=z, it is **logical** to say:
a. 7+y = z+7
b. x=y
c. x+y=z

_____ 5. Write an **original** poem about happiness.

_____ 6. How tall are you? **Measure** your height and give your answer in feet / inches.

_____ 7. **Solve** the following problem for x:
$5(-3x - 2) - (x - 3) = -4(4x + 5) + 13$

_____ 8. Your soccer team lost the first three games. What can you say to yourself and your team to **encourage** them to play better?

_____ 9. **Prove** that two sides of the triangle below are equal:

Academic Subjects

a. Physical Education (sports)

b. History

c. Math or Geometry

d. English

2 Look back at the boldfaced words in the Sample Test Questions on the previous page. Then match the words on the left with the definitions on the right.

_f_ **1.** focus on (something)   **a.** making sense

____ **2.** logical   **b.** to make (something)

____ **3.** fact   **c.** not copied; one of a kind

____ **4.** measure (something)   **d.** to find the answer to (something)

____ **5.** prove (something)   **e.** to show that (something) is true

____ **6.** original   ~~**f.** to pay very close attention to (something)~~

____ **7.** encourage (someone)   **g.** a statement that is true

____ **8.** create (something)   **h.** to find out the size (of something)

____ **9.** solve (something)   **i.** to say and do things to help (someone) do well

■■■■■■■■■■■■■■■■■■■■■■■■■■■■■■■■ GO TO MyEnglishLab FOR MORE VOCABULARY PRACTICE.

PREVIEW

You are going to read a magazine article about teaching creative thinking. From your experience, do schools teach creative thinking? In which classes are students most likely to learn creative thinking skills? Check (✓) the appropriate classes.

❑ Math class
❑ Art class
❑ History class
❑ Science class
❑ English class

Now read the article.

CAN WE TEACH CREATIVE THINKING IN SCHOOLS?

By Martha Maddux

Steve Jobs **created** *the iPod.*

Lady Gaga writes hit songs.

Mom made a delicious dinner with the food she found in the refrigerator.

Uncle Fred fixed our broken car with a can opener.

Lady Gaga

1   These creative people all did important things. Some people were famous and they changed history; others were not well known and they only helped one family for a day.

2   None of the people on the list finished college. Many of the world's most creative thinkers learned their creative skills *outside* of school.

3   Creative thinking is a very important skill. It helps us make new things. It also helps us solve everyday problems that don't have one easy answer. Yet traditional schools often don't **encourage** creative thinking. Many teachers don't know how to teach it or **measure** it.

4   Schools like to **prove** that students are learning. So they usually **focus on** teaching **logical** thinking and **facts**, which are easy to measure.

5   In contrast, creative thinking results in **original** answers—new answers that others don't usually think of. $2 + 2 = 4$ if you are counting houses or apples. But if a student is counting 2 hungry foxes[1] + 2 fat chickens, then $2+2 = 2$ happy foxes.

6   Most people think creative thinking is difficult to understand. They think it is hard to teach. They think they can't measure or grade it. But it is not so complicated. Creative thinking is putting different ideas together in new ways.

7   Some skilled teachers teach creative thinking all the time, in addition to teaching facts. They might teach students to measure the size of a room and also have them describe the size of a room ("It's the size of a racquetball court"; Or "It's big enough for a salsa band to practice"). They might teach facts about history and also have students discuss possible meanings of a painting from that time ("The red colors seem angry, and that is how people were feeling during that revolution"). They might even tell students to create stories about when $2+2$ does not equal 4!

8   Measuring creative thinking is not easy, but it is possible. There is no one right or wrong answer to a creative thinking question. How can a teacher (or a computer!) know if "$2+2 = 2$" is a creative answer about foxes and

$2 + 2 = $ _____ ○ 0 ○ 2 ● 4 ○ 8	Mahatma Ghandi . . . ○ was an English politician. ● led India to independence. ○ is the current president of India.	Yesterday, Youssef _____ his first year at university. ● began ○ begin ○ have begun ○ begun

Examples of traditional test questions that have right and wrong answers.

---

[1] **fox:** a wild animal, similar to a dog

chickens, or if it is simply a wrong answer? Teachers need to see students' reasons for their answers in order to measure creative thinking. The student with the creative answer to 2+2 is putting math together with her knowledge from English class. She just read a novel about farming and learned about foxes and chickens. Another student might say "2+2 = 2 because I like the number two!" That is not creative thinking.

9   Can schools teach creative thinking? Absolutely! And they *must*! Teaching **logical** thinking and facts is still important. We need math skills to make sure we don't spend more money than we have, for example. But many other questions in life do not have clear right and wrong answers. For example, how do you feed a family healthy food with only a small amount of money? Our schools need to prepare students for those tasks as well. Teaching creative thinking to our students helps them to **solve** more problems, and that helps the rest of us. The world needs creative thinkers to create the next iPod. But we also need them to make dinner.

MAIN IDEAS

1 Look again at the Preview on page 29. How did your answers help you understand the article?

2 Check (✓) the statement that best describes the main idea of the article.

_____ **a.** You need to leave school to learn creative thinking skills.

_____ **b.** Math teachers need to teach more creative thinking because sometimes math has many interesting answers.

_____ **c.** Schools can and must teach creative skills because the world needs creative thinkers.

_____ **d.** Creative people should become teachers so that we can have more creative teaching in our schools.

DETAILS

Cross out the incorrect ending to each statement.

1. Creative skills are important because _____.

   a. they help us make new things

   b. they help us solve everyday problems

   c. they help us learn math better

2. Schools often don't teach creative thinking because _____.

   a. students don't want to learn creative thinking

   b. teachers don't know how to teach it

   c. creative thinking is difficult to measure

3. Creative thinking _____.

   a. is impossible to understand

   b. is putting ideas together in new ways

   c. results in original answers

4. Creative thinking questions _____.

   a. usually have one correct answer

   b. have many possible answers

   c. ask you to put information together in new ways

MAKE INFERENCES

INFERRING CONNECTIONS BETWEEN GENERAL STATEMENTS AND EXAMPLES

An **inference** is an educated guess about something that is not directly stated in the text. Writers often use examples to help readers understand a general statement. Sometimes readers need to **infer** the connection between a general statement (or definition) and an example in a text.

Look at the general statement and example and read the explanation.

- **General statement:** Creative thinking is putting different ideas together in new ways.

- **Example:** It's [the room is] the size of a racquetball court. *(paragraph 7)*

In this example of creative thinking, the student puts different ideas together in new ways: He describes the size of a room by putting together his knowledge of math and sports.

After reading the example closely, we can **infer** its connection with the general statement, and we get a better understanding of what creative thinking is.

Look at each example of creative thinking from the text and answer the question. Choose subjects from the box.

Art	English	History	Music
Business	Health	Math	Science

EXAMPLE OF CREATIVE THINKING	WHAT SUBJECT KNOWLEDGE DOES THE STUDENT PUT TOGETHER?
1. It's [the room is] big enough for a salsa band to practice. (paragraph 7)	
2. The red colors seem angry, and that is how people were feeling during that revolution. (paragraph 7)	
3. Trying to feed a family healthy food with only a small amount of money. (paragraph 9)	

Now discuss your answers with a partner.

EXPRESS OPINIONS

Discuss the questions below with a partner. Give your opinions. Then share your answers with the class.

1. The article states that most schools focus on teaching logical thinking and facts, not creative thinking. Was this true in your school? Give examples of things you did in school. Did you learn logical or creative thinking?

2. Do you agree that it is important to teach creative thinking in schools? Which of the author's reasons do you agree or disagree with? What other reasons do you have for your opinion?

■■■■■■■■■■■■■■■■■■■■■■ *GO TO* MyEnglishLab *TO GIVE YOUR OPINION ABOUT ANOTHER QUESTION.*

READ

1 Look at the boldfaced words and phrases in the reading and think about these questions.

1. Which words or phrases do you know the meanings of?

2. Can you use any of the words or phrases in a sentence?

2 Now read the page from a "Skills for success in college" website.

Tips for Success in College: How to Be Creative

1 As you begin college, you will receive lots of advice about how to be a good student; for example, always attend your classes, be organized, and get to know your teachers. This is all great advice, and it will certainly help you to succeed in your classes. But there is another kind of advice that is less common: advice to help you *use* what you learn in your classes to make something new and original!

2 The following tips may be the most important ones that you get: Tips on how to be creative.

Be curious

3 This is the most important tip, and there are so many ways to do it: If you walk the same way to school every day, take another path. List three classes that you don't know anything about at your school. Then take one. When your roommate invites you to a cricket match, say "YES!" Even if you don't know anything about cricket, go and learn about it.

A cricket match

Being **curious** helps us learn new things. The more things we know about, the more possibilities we have for combining information in original ways. One common definition of creative thinking is **combining** information in new ways.

Take risks

4   Many of us are afraid of **taking risks** because we are afraid of making mistakes. This fear may come from parents or others who say, for example: "You are not very good at singing—you should keep quiet" or "I'm afraid you'll do it wrong." Stop listening to those people. Never fear making mistakes. Try out your Spanish with a native speaker! Write a song, even if you are not sure how to do it. Learn a new sport. Thomas Edison's first light bulbs didn't work. They were mistakes, but each one gave him the information he needed to create a light bulb that worked. Creative people take risks, but you won't take risks if you are afraid of making mistakes.

Whatever you create, make a lot of it

5   Write lots of stories. Draw lots of pictures. Build lots of models. A **study** compared work from two college ceramics classes. One teacher told students, "make as many **pieces** as you can." The other teacher told students, "make the best piece you can." You can guess where the best work was—in the class where students made lots of pieces.

A ceramics class

COMPREHENSION

Complete the sentence by checking (✓) all possible endings.

In order to be creative you should:

_____ **a.** Follow the tips on the website.

_____ **b.** Stop going to your regular classes.

_____ **c.** Learn about many different subjects.

_____ **d.** Learn from mistakes.

_____ **e.** Be very careful in everything you do.

_____ **f.** Focus on one long project at a time.

GO TO MyEnglishLab *FOR MORE VOCABULARY PRACTICE.*

READING SKILL

1 Read paragraph 3 of Reading Two again. The title of that paragraph is "Be curious." How many examples of specific ways to be curious can you find in that paragraph? Underline them.

RECOGNIZING EXAMPLES

Examples help readers understand the general idea in a text. Usually in English, the writer gives the general idea (statement) first, then the specific examples. Sometimes the writer introduces examples with the words *for example*.

General statement:

- Be curious.

Specific examples:

- If you walk the same way to school every day, take another path.
- List three classes you know nothing about at your school. Then take one.
- When your roommate invites you to a cricket match, say "YES!"

2 Read paragraphs 4 and 5 of Reading Two again. Each paragraph has a general statement and several examples. Write them in this e-chart.

Paragraph 4

_____

general statement

Paragraph 5

_____

general statement

| _____ |
| example 1 |
| _____ |
| example 2 |
| _____ |
| example 3 |

Now discuss these questions with a partner.

1. How many examples are in each paragraph?

2. Do they help you understand the general statement?

GO TO MyEnglishLab FOR MORE SKILL PRACTICE.

STEP 1: Organize

Look at Reading One (**R1**) and Reading Two (**R2**) again. Choose phrases from the list to complete the chart. The example answer is the only one that uses a phrase twice.

- take risks
- whatever you create, make a lot of it
- logical thinking and facts
- helps us make new things [and] solve everyday problems that don't have one easy answer
- college students

- be curious
- schools
- ~~teach creative thinking~~
- ~~combining ideas in new ways~~
- help you use what you learn in your classes to make something new and original

	READING ONE (R1)	READING TWO (R2)
1. Definition of creative thinking	*combining ideas in new ways*	*combining ideas in new ways*
2. Opposite of creative thinking		✕
3. Why is creative thinking important?		
4. Who or what needs to change?		
5. What should they do?	*teach creative thinking*	a. _____ b. _____ c. _____

STEP 2: Synthesize

Use ideas from the chart above, as well as your own ideas, to complete the conversation between Kristin and Joshua, two engineering students.

JOSHUA: My design class is making me crazy. I think I'm going to drop it.

KRISTIN: But you are an engineering major! You have to take design.

JOSHUA: I know. But I don't understand what Professor Sousa wants me to do. I'm getting lots of Cs.

(continued on next page)

KRISTIN: Professor Sousa's class was also hard for me at first. He teaches some
logical thinking and facts, but he also wants you to learn creative thinking.

JOSHUA: But I am not an artist!

KRISTIN: Creative thinking is important in *all* subjects, not just art. We need to learn creative
thinking because _____

_____.

JOSHUA: But I don't have time to learn creative thinking! We have to make 25 drawings
every day!

KRISTIN: That is a perfect example of one "how to be creative" tip! To become more creative,
you should: _____. I think
Professor Sousa knows this.

He doesn't give you bad grades for *bad* drawings. He gives you bad grades for *not
enough* drawings.

JOSHUA: Really? So if I just make lots drawings, I am becoming more creative and getting
better grades?

KRISTIN: Exactly. Another tip for becoming more creative is: _____.
For example, _____.

JOSHUA: I see. This is helpful. What else did you learn?

KRISTIN: The last tip is: _____.
For example, _____.

JOSHUA: I think I am beginning to understand. Thank you, Kris.

■■■■■■■■■■■■■■■■■■■■■■■■■■■■■■■■■■■■■■■ *GO TO* MyEnglishLab *TO CHECK WHAT YOU LEARNED.*

VOCABULARY

REVIEW

Complete the sentences with the correct words or phrases from the box.

~~combining~~	fact	original	study
create	focus on	pieces	take a risk
curious	logical	prove	
encourage	measure	solve	

1. My favorite class is History and Literature of the American Revolution. _____Combining_____ English and History in one class is a great idea!

2. Tell me more about your life. I am _____.

3. I know you think you are a terrible dancer. _____ and sign up for the class anyway!

4. Being bored can help you be more creative. That is what a recent _____ at the University of Central Lancashire found.

5. Each art student painted six _____ for the final.

6. Michelle hates numbers, but she became a math teacher? That's not _____.

7. You may not like online education, but it is a _____ that more students are taking classes online every year.

8. Steve just made a CD of 14 _____ songs. He is a great songwriter!

9. My roommate is not doing well in his classes. We need to _____ him to do better.

10. For Creative Writing class, I have to _____ a blog. I will put my writing there, and other students can comment on it.

11. My advisor tells me I have to _____ one major. But I can't decide. I love studying all different things!

(continued on next page)

12. Our baseball team got new shoes, but they were the wrong sizes. The coach forgot to _____ our feet before he ordered them!

13. I need to take the English entrance test tomorrow. If I _____ I can write an essay, I don't have to take English 1A.

14. Ben, can you help me _____ this problem? I can't get the computer to work with the projector.

EXPAND

1 Read the sentences on the left, paying attention to the boldfaced expressions. Then match the sentences on the left with the sentences that have similar meanings on the right.

_____ **1.** I **solved the problem**.

_____ **2.** I **had an idea**.

_____ **3.** I **realized** Pam was an artist.

_____ **4.** I **remembered** Pam was an artist.

_____ **5.** That film **made me think of** Pam.

a. This was always true, but I only just understood it.

b. I knew this, but I forgot until now.

c. First, it was difficult, but then I found an answer that worked.

d. I thought of something new.

e. I saw it and I thought of her.

2 Now complete each sentence with the appropriate boldfaced expression from the sentences above.

1. I saw the beautiful weather yesterday morning. Then I _____. I called some friends, and we had a picnic at the beach.

2. I didn't understand what that woman said to me at first. Then I _____ she was speaking Dutch, not English.

3. I thought there was nothing in the house for lunch. Then I _____ I had bought a frozen pizza last week.

4. I heard a new band called Japandroids today. They _____ you. I think you will like them.

5. We lost our electricity on Christmas Day last year. At first, it was terrible! But we _____. We cooked dinner on the barbecue, and we used candles for light.

CREATE

Use the vocabulary and expressions in parentheses to complete the conversations between freshman students in the Student Lounge Discussion Area. For the last question, use new vocabulary from the unit. Your partner will try to answer your question.

STUDENT LOUNGE DISCUSSION AREA
Use this discussion area to get to know each other and to ask each other for advice about your classes.

Valencia Scott 4:45pm March 24, 2013

Hey everyone! Help! I am having trouble in ENG 145. We have to write research papers. I went to a high school for the arts. We wrote lots of poetry and stories, but this seems completely different. Any advice?

_____ (your name) 7:32pm March 24, 2013

(logical thinking / facts / studies)

Hi Valencia! Yes, ENG 145 essays are not very creative. I learned to write research papers in high school, though, so I understand

them. Try to use _____. _____

_____

_____

Shakeam Clements 2:31am March 25, 2013

Is anyone having the same problem as me? I want to study art, but my counselor tells me I have to also study math and history. I am in college now, and I want to do what I want! Why do I need to take all these other classes that are not about art?

_____ (your name) 11:05am March 25, 2013

(focus on / curious / realize / combine)

Hey Shakeam: I used to ask the same question. Math and history are super important for artists, too!

Try to _____. _____

_____

_____

_____

(continued on next page)

_____ (your name) 11:25am March 25, 2013

Can anyone help me solve this problem? _____

_____

_____

_____

GO TO MyEnglishLab FOR MORE VOCABULARY PRACTICE.

GRAMMAR

1 Read the paragraph. Underline the verbs that tell about the past. Then answer the questions.

My mother helped me learn to keep working on problems. She always told me, "There are no mistakes, only lessons." In my first year of college, I failed math. I wanted to quit college. When she talked to me, I remembered all of the reasons for going to college. We looked at my math tests and homework together. She helped me see which things were most difficult for me. When I took math again, I went to extra study sessions. And I passed with a B+!

1. How is the simple past formed for most verbs (regular verbs)?

2. Which past tense verbs are irregular? What is the base form of each one of these verbs?

SIMPLE PAST TENSE

1. When we talk about things that happened in the past, we use the **simple past tense**.	My mother **helped** me. I **went** to extra study sessions.	
	Base Form	Simple Past
2. To form the simple past tense for **regular** verbs, add **-ed** to the base form of the verb.	help talk	help**ed** talk**ed**
If the verb ends in **-e**, add only **-d**.	live arrive	live**d** arrive**d**
If the verb ends in a consonant + **y**, change the **y** to **i** and then add **-ed**.	study try	stud**ied** tr**ied**

3. Many verbs have **irregular** past tense forms.
Here are some of these irregular verbs.

Base Form	Simple Past
be	**was / were**
begin	**began**
come	**came**
do	**did**
have	**had**
get	**got**
go	**went**
make	**made**
meet	**met**
say	**said**
take	**took**
think	**thought**
write	**wrote**

4. In negative statements, use:
didn't (did not) + base form of the verb, except with the verb *be.*

Base Form	Simple Past
need	**didn't** need
go	**didn't** go
be	**wasn't / weren't**

2 Complete the student's blog about his first week at art school, using the simple past tense forms of the verbs in parentheses.

○ ○ ○

Andreas's Art Adventures

HOME

CONTACT

ABOUT ME

Hello everyone!

My dream _____*came*_____ true! I am now a student at the University of Art
1. (come)
and Design!

Classes _____ one week ago. I am sorry for the group email, but
2. (begin)
I am so busy!

Here are a few highlights from my first week:

• I _____ my department head. He _____ at
3. (meet)   4. (work)
Disney for many years!

(continued on next page)

He _____ that art school is a lot of hard work. (He
     5. (say)

_____ right.)
     6. (be)

- I _____ to my first
       7. (go)
drawing class and _____
                     8. (practice)
drawing ellipses for one hour! I think I

_____ 500! I am getting
       9. (make)
better, but my teacher says they are still not good enough.

ellipses

- I _____ figure drawing homework for 15 hours on Sunday!
       10. (do)

- I _____ my favorite artist (Andy Warhol) and
       11. (research)

_____ a paper about him.
       12. (write)

- I _____ of 25 ways to use a paperclip. (I don't know
       13. (think)
why we _____ this, but I will find out this week.)
             14. (do)

- I _____ a song and _____ it for my
       15. (write)   16. (play)
English class.

(I _____ excited about this, but I _____ a risk!!)
       17. (not / be)   18. (take)

- I _____ the names, dates, and artists of 25 Renaissance
       19. (learn)
paintings.

- I _____ much!
       20. (not / sleep)
Thank you all for your emails and messages! I will try to post again soon.
Andreas

3 Read a page of Cory's application for college. Complete the sentences in the simple past tense. Choose the correct verb from the box. One verb will be used twice.

Application p. 1

Name: Cory Hansen   **Date of birth:** January 27, 1995

Schools and dates
Crocker Elementary School	September 2000–June 2006
Jerry Brown Middle School	September 2006–June 2009
Oakland Technical High School	September 2009–June 2013
De Anza Community College	January 2014–present

Last semester's classes and final grades
English	A
Spanish	A–
Biology	B

Clubs
Boy Scouts of America 2007–2009
Oakland Tech Chess Club 2009–2012

Sports
Oakland Tech Varsity Football 2011–2013

attend	get	join	start
~~finish~~	go	play	

1. Cory _____finished_____ high school in June 2013.

2. He (not) _____ to school from June 2013 until January 2014.

3. He _____ taking classes at De Anza Community College in January 2014.

4. He _____ an A in English

5. He (not) _____ an A in Biology.

6. He _____ the Boy Scouts of America in 2007.

7. He _____ Jerry Brown Middle School from 2006 until 2009.

8. He _____ varsity football for Oakland Tech from 2011 until 2013.

■■■■■■■■■■■ GO TO MyEnglishLab FOR MORE GRAMMAR PRACTICE AND TO CHECK WHAT YOU LEARNED.

FINAL WRITING TASK

In this unit, you read about the differences between creative thinking and logical thinking. You also read some suggestions for how to be creative.

Now you are going to *write a paragraph about a time you (or someone you know) used creative thinking to solve a problem.* Introduce the story. Describe the problem. Tell how you (or someone else) used creative thinking (being curious, combining ideas, taking risks, making a lot of something) to solve it. Use the vocabulary and grammar from the unit.*

PREPARE TO WRITE: Charting a Writing Prompt

Charting your writing prompt can help you make sure you answer all the parts of a question when you write. The chart below has one row for each part of the question you will answer in your paragraph.

1. Introduce the story	*Being curious helped me solve a big problem for my grandfather.*
2. Describe the problem	*My grandfather can't type emails or texts because he has very shaky hands.*
3. Tell how you (or someone else) used creative thinking (being curious, combining ideas, taking risks, making a lot of something) to solve it.	*I was curious about iPads because so many people love them.* *I found the VoiceText app.* *It made me think of my grandfather.*

Look at the chart and think about a time you or someone else used creative thinking to solve a problem. The problem might be a difficult assignment in school, or it might be an everyday problem. Complete the chart. Then discuss your answers with a partner.

1. Introduce the story	
2. Describe the problem	
3. Tell how you (or someone else) used creative thinking (being curious, combining ideas, taking risks, making a lot of something) to solve it.	

---

* For Alternative Writing Topics, see page 53. These topics can be used in place of the writing topic for this unit or as homework. The alternative topics relate to the theme of the unit but may not target the same grammar or rhetorical structures taught in the unit.

WRITING A COMPLETE PARAGRAPH

A complete paragraph has **three parts:** a topic sentence, supporting sentences, and a conclusion. In this assignment, do the following in each part:

- **Topic sentence:** Introduce the topic and make a general statement. (This may be one or two sentences.)
- **Supporting sentences:** Explain the problem and the creative process you introduced in the topic sentence.
- **Conclusion:** Tell the end of the story, or make a final comment about the story.

1 Read the paragraph. Put brackets [ ] around the three parts of the paragraph.

Being curious helped me solve a big problem for my grandfather. He can't type emails or texts because he has very shaky hands. I was curious about iPads because so many people love them. I borrowed my friend's iPad and looked at all the games and other apps on the screen. I played a few games and learned about a few apps. But the best app was VoiceText. I touched it, I talked, then all of my words came on the screen. It was like someone else was typing my words! It made me think of my grandfather. He can't type, but he can talk! My cousins and I bought him an iPad with VoiceText, and now he can text or email us any time!

(continued on next page)

2 Each paragraph is missing one part. Circle the name of the part it is missing.

Paragraph 1

Last semester in English, I took a big risk and wrote a very creative essay about my grandmother. My teacher loved it and told me it was very creative. After that, I began to take more risks in my writing. Now I am a better writer, and I also enjoy it more.

What is missing?

    a. Topic sentence

    b. Supporting sentences

    c. Conclusion

Paragraph 2

My history teacher last semester used a very creative way to teach our class. During the first class, she got angry with students because they looked at their phones during class. For the second class, she asked who had Twitter accounts. Half of the class raised their hands. She put us in pairs so that each pair had a phone with a Twitter account. She told us to search for the hashtag #hist232 in Twitter. We did, and we found a history question from her! We discussed the question with our partners, then tweeted the answer with the hashtag #hist232. We looked at all our answers on the big screen at the front of the class. We had interesting conversations with each other on Twitter and in person.

What is missing?

    a. Topic sentence

    b. Supporting sentences

    c. Conclusion

3 Now write the first draft of your paragraph about a time you (or someone else) used creative thinking to solve a problem. Start with your topic sentence, explain the problem and the process, and then finish with a conclusion. Use the ideas in your chart on page 46 to help you write your paragraph.

REVISE: Using Your Creative Skills

Sometimes words do not communicate the whole message in a piece of writing. **Visuals** like pictures or charts can be useful, too. As you revise, use your creative skills, like including visuals, to communicate better with your readers. Combine writing with another skill that you have. Take a risk!

1 Read the revisions of the paragraphs and finish the sentence below each one.

Paragraph 1

Being curious helped me solve a big problem for my grandfather. He can't type emails or texts because he has very shaky hands. I was curious about iPads because so many people love them. I borrowed my friend's iPad and looked at all the games and other apps on the screen. I played a few games and learned about a few apps. But the best app was VoiceText. I touched it, I talked, then all of my words came on the screen. It was like someone else was typing my words! It made me think of my grandfather. He can't type, but he can talk! My cousins and I bought him an iPad with VoiceText, and now he can text or email us any time!

The picture gives the reader more information about _____.

Paragraph 2

My history teacher last semester used a very creative way to teach our class. During the first class, she got angry with students because they looked at their phones during class. For the second class, she asked who had Twitter accounts. Half of the class raised their hands. She put us in pairs so that each pair had a phone with a Twitter account. She told us to search for the hashtag #hist232 in Twitter. We did, and we found a history question from her! We discussed the question with our partners, then

tweeted the answer with the hashtag #hist232. We looked at all our answers on the big screen at the front of the class. We had interesting conversations with each other on Twitter and in person. This teacher combined her knowledge of history, Twitter, and young students to create that fun exercise. After that day, history was always fun, and the teacher didn't get angry anymore.

The picture gives the reader more information about _____.

2 Work with a partner. Read the paragraph. Then discuss the two questions.

A man in Denmark used creative thinking to get a job. Getting a job is often a big problem to solve. This man wrote his name and a short résumé in the snow in a parking lot. Then he lay down on the ground next to the résumé. The people in the office building looked out the window and saw him with his résumé. I think he took a big risk! Usually people dress very well for job interviews, and they make their résumés look very professional. I don't know if he got a job, but his idea was very original.

1. What will the reader be curious to know more about?
2. What can the writer add to give the reader more information?

3 Now go back to the first draft of your paragraph. What will your reader be curious to know more about? What can you add to give more information? Revise your paragraph and add something creative (like visuals) to help your reader understand your message.

■■■■■■■■■■■■■■■■■■■■■■■■■■■■■■■ *GO TO* MyEnglishLab *FOR MORE SKILL PRACTICE.*

EDIT: Writing the Final Draft

Go to MyEnglishLab and write the final draft of your paragraph. Carefully edit it for grammatical and mechanical errors, such as spelling, capitalization, and punctuation. Make sure you use some of the vocabulary and grammar from the unit. Use the checklist to help you write your final draft. Then submit your paragraph to your teacher.

FINAL DRAFT CHECKLIST

❑ Does your paragraph tell about a time you or someone else used creative thinking?

❑ Does it have a topic sentence?

❑ Does it have supporting sentences that tell about the problem, and the creative thinking process?

❑ Does it have a conclusion that finishes the story or adds a comment to the story?

❑ Does it have a picture, chart, or other element that helps the reader understand the message better?

❑ Do you use past tense verbs correctly?

❑ Do you use new vocabulary that you learned in this unit?

UNIT PROJECT

Work in small groups. Create a "Guide to Original Weekend Activities in [your town or area]." Your guide will only include original ideas, not the ones that everyone already knows about. It can be useful for people who live in your town or for people who visit. You need to use your creative thinking skills! Follow these steps:

STEP 1: (Do this several days before Step 2.) List three to five things to see or do in your town that you have never done. You can go online to get ideas. Then go and do them! (Be curious! Take risks!)

STEP 2: List at least ten fun things to do in your town on the weekends. (Don't worry about being original yet. Just list a lot of things. You can only list things that you have actually done!)

STEP 3: In your group, look at your lists together. If more than one other person wrote the same thing on their list, everyone crosses that thing out. (Find original ideas.)

Example

What are fun things to do on the weekend in Jackson?

Hyun
Hike to Indian Grinding Rock
Bicycle on the river path
Take a tour of the candy factory
Get ice cream at Wierschem's
Play volleyball at Detert Park
    on Saturday afternoon
Go to the museum

Claudia
Hike to Indian Grinding Rock
Go to the museum
Bike on the river path
Get ice cream at
    Wierschem's
Swim across the river at
    Bud's dock

Hussein
Visit the candy factory
Walk on Indian Grinding
    Rock
Go to the museum
Get Wierschem's ice
    cream to eat

STEP 4: Make a final list for your "Guide to Original Weekend Activities in
_____." You might include some additional information such as
admission price, opening hours, and address. Share your list with other groups.

ALTERNATIVE WRITING TOPICS

Write about one of the topics below. Use the vocabulary and grammar from the unit.

1. Write a paragraph about a time you made a big mistake. Did you fear mistakes afterwards, or did you learn from your mistake?

2. Write a paragraph about someone you know who is very creative. Give examples of why you think he or she is creative. Does he or she do the things suggested in Reading Two? What else does this person do?

3. Did you learn creative thinking in school? Write a paragraph about it. Give some examples of how you did or didn't learn it. How did those experiences affect you today?

■■■■■■■■■■■■ GO TO MyEnglishLab TO WRITE ABOUT ONE OF THE ALTERNATIVE TOPICS, WATCH A VIDEO ABOUT CREATIVITY, AND TAKE THE UNIT 2 ACHIEVEMENT TEST. ■■■■■■■■■■■■■■■■■■■■■■■■■■■■■■■■■■

MAKING
Money

1 FOCUS ON THE TOPIC

1. Copying money becomes easier as copier technology becomes better. What equipment do people need to copy money?

2. What is the best way to stop people from copying money?

3. How can you tell real money from copied (fake) money?

GO TO MyEnglishLab TO CHECK WHAT YOU KNOW.

2 FOCUS ON READING

VOCABULARY

When you read a story, there may be many words you don't know. Often you can still understand the story, and sometimes you can even understand these new words.

1 Read the story. See if you can understand it even though some words are missing.

One day last year, some New York City sanitation workers were very surprised when they emptied a garbage can. Along with the banana peels and empty Coke cans, they found $18 million in new _____.
                                                          1.

Who would throw out all that money? The workers felt that something was not right, so they called the United States Bureau of Engraving and Printing, the part of government that makes paper money. The Bureau employees said that the money looked real but that, in fact, it wasn't. It was _____—and not legal. The garbage must have belonged to
                        2.
_____, people who make money that is not real. They use both old and new
        3.
_____, or ways, to make money. For example, some make the money by using
        4.
printing presses, big machines similar to those for making books or newspapers; others use _____ and other computer _____. These counterfeiters probably
        5.   6.
printed a lot of money and weren't happy with how it looked. Maybe the drawing wasn't good enough. Or maybe the _____ was not exactly the right color. So they threw it
                            7.
all out.

The people at the Bureau of Engraving and Printing were mad. Copying money is _____. Counterfeiters who get caught can go to prison for a long time. The people
        8.
at the Bureau work very hard to _____ people from making fake money.
                                    9.

The Bureau never caught these counterfeiters. Nobody knows if they were able to make another $18 million that looked _____ real.
                                        10.

Now answer the questions. Then discuss your answers with a classmate.

1. What did the New York City sanitation workers find?

_____

2. Who threw out all that money?

_____

2 Read the story again. Work with a partner. Use information in the story to guess the missing words. Write your guesses on the lines.

3 Now read the list of words and their definitions. Then read the story again and use these words to complete it. Write the new vocabulary words above your own guesses.

> **bills:** pieces of paper money
>
> **completely:** 100 percent
>
> **counterfeiters:** people who make money that is not real
>
> **equipment:** machines and tools used to make other things
>
> **fake:** not real
>
> **illegal:** not legal; against the law
>
> **ink:** a colored liquid in pens and printers, used for writing and printing
>
> **prevent:** stop something from happening before it happens
>
> **scanners:** machines that copy pictures from paper onto a computer
>
> **technologies:** ways to make things, usually with some kind of machine

■■■■■■■■■■■■■■■■■■■■■■ *GO TO* MyEnglishLab *FOR MORE VOCABULARY PRACTICE.*

PREVIEW

The following magazine article is about how some counterfeiters make fake money. It is also about how the U.S. government tries to stop counterfeiting.

Work in a small group. Make a list of things that you think the government might do to make money harder to copy.

1. _____

2. _____

3. _____

4. _____

5. _____

Now read the article "Making Money."

MAKING MONEY

By Amelia Laidlaw

1   IT WAS SO QUICK AND EASY. A 14-year-old boy in Scottsdale, Arizona, pulled out a $50 **bill** and put it onto his school's new **scanner**. Then he printed ten copies of his $50 bill on a color copier. Within seconds he changed $50 into $550, and he was ready to go shopping.

2   Thirty years ago only a few people had the skills or **equipment** to make counterfeit money. Good computers, copiers, cameras, and printers are cheaper than ever, so today anyone can "make" money. The people using today's **technology** to make fake money are called casual **counterfeiters**, and like the 14-year-old in Arizona, they can be anywhere.

3   The number of **fake** bills made by casual counterfeiters on their home or office computer is growing fast. Although there is no way to **completely prevent** counterfeiting, in the 1990s and 2000s, the U.S. government made some changes to U.S. bills that made casual counterfeiting more difficult.

4   One change they made was to put very, very small words, called microprint, in hidden places on the bill. These words are only 6/1,000 inch. No one can read them without a magnifying glass, a special glass that makes things look bigger. And they are too small to come out clearly on a copier. If someone copies a bill that has microprint and you look at the copy through a magnifying glass, you see only black lines instead of microprinted words.

5   Another change the government made to U.S. bills was to use special color-changing **ink**. Money printed with color-changing ink looks green from one direction and yellow from another. Home computers cannot use color-changing ink. So any **illegal** copies of money from a home computer have normal ink that is easy to notice.

6   The third change was to add a special line from the top to the bottom of each new bill. When you hold a $20 bill up to the light for example, you can see the line has the words "USA twenty" in it. The line turns red if you put it under a special UV (ultraviolet) light. Fake bills printed on regular paper do not have this special line. You can tell they are fake by holding them up to the light or by putting them under UV light.

7   All these changes to the U.S. bills help. The United States has less counterfeit money than any other country in the world. Less than 1% of U.S. money is counterfeit. However, the Bureau of Engraving and Printing can't slow down now because of these changes. It needs to always stay a step or two ahead of the counterfeiters. Already, the Bureau has plans to add a 3D image to the U.S. $100 bill. This is something they hope will be impossible to copy. But technology improves every year. Today, home copiers can't copy microprinted words or 3D images. But in a few years, who knows?

MAIN IDEAS

1 Look again at the Preview on page 57. How did your predictions help you understand the article?

2 Each statement tells the main idea of a paragraph in "Making Money." Read a statement, then write the correct paragraph number next to it.

Paragraph

a. Casual counterfeiting is becoming a big problem, and the government is fighting the problem. _____

b. Using color-changing ink is a way to prevent counterfeiting. _____

c. A child can easily copy paper money. _____

d. The government must always keep changing the bills to prevent counterfeiting. _____

e. Putting microprint on bills helps prevent counterfeiting. _____

f. New technology makes casual counterfeiting possible. _____

g. The special lines on U.S. paper money help prevent counterfeiting. _____

3 Check (✓) the statement that best describes the main idea of the whole article.

_____ **a.** It's easier to counterfeit money today than it was 30 years ago, especially with the right equipment.

_____ **b.** The government has several ways to try to prevent counterfeiting.

_____ **c.** Better home computers and printers made counterfeiting easier, so the U.S. government changed the bills to make counterfeiting more difficult.

DETAILS

Complete the statements with information from the article.

1. Thirty years ago, only a few people had the _____ or _____

to make fake money.

2. One way to prevent counterfeiters from making fake money on a _____

is to use microprinted words.

3. Bills have a _____ that you can see if you hold them up to the light.

(continued on next page)

Making Money 59

4. A boy in Scottsdale, Arizona, used his school's scanner to make _____

copies of a $_____ bill.

5. Money printed with color-changing ink looks green from one direction and

_____ from another.

6. Most other countries in the world have _____ counterfeit money than

the United States.

MAKE INFERENCES

INFERRING FUTURE SITUATIONS

An **inference** is an educated guess about something that is not directly stated in the text. Readers often use information in a text to infer what will happen in the future.

Look at the example and read the explanation.

• In the future, more people will make fake money.

Is this true? Choose the best answer.

a. Probably true, based on what we read in the article.

b. There is not enough information in the article to know if this statement is true.
   *(The best answer is **a**.)*

In paragraph 2, we learn that anyone with basic computer equipment can be a counterfeiter.
In paragraph 3, we learn that the number of counterfeit bills grows every year.
In paragraph 7, we learn that technology improves every year.

So, from all this information, we can **infer** that **in the future**, the number of casual counterfeiters will continue to grow because it's easy, and computers are getting cheaper and better.

Read each prediction. Can you tell if it is true or not from the information in the article? Choose the best answer. Refer to the paragraphs in parentheses.

1. Copiers will not be able to copy color-changing ink. *(paragraphs 5 and 7)*

   a. True, based on what we read in the article.

   b. There is not enough information in the article to know if this statement is true.

2. Copiers will be able to copy microprinted words. *(paragraph 7)*

   a. True, based on what we read in the article.

   b. There is not enough information in the article to know if this statement is true.

3. The Bureau of Engraving and Printing will learn about new home computer technology before people buy it. *(paragraph 7)*

   a. True, based on what we read in the article.

   b. There is not enough information in the article to know if this statement is true.

4. The police will be able to catch most counterfeiters. *(paragraph 7)*

   a. True, based on what we read in the article.

   b. There is not enough information in the article to know if this statement is true.

Now discuss your answers with a partner. Explain your thinking.

EXPRESS OPINIONS

Discuss the questions in a small group. Give your opinions. Then share your answers with the class.

1. Review the changes the U.S. government made to bills to prevent people from counterfeiting. Which of them seems the most effective to you? Why?

2. What else can the Bureau of Engraving and Printing do to stay a step ahead of casual counterfeiters?

■■■■■■■■■■■■■■■■■■■■■■■ *GO TO* MyEnglishLab *TO GIVE YOUR OPINION ABOUT ANOTHER QUESTION.*

READING TWO   I MADE IT MYSELF

READ

Before computers and copiers, counterfeiting was not easy. You needed the artistic skill to draw a copy of a bill, a large printing press, and the skill to use it. Counterfeiting often took a lot of time, planning, and hard work. And the results were excellent. The counterfeit money looked and felt like the real thing. Today, professional counterfeiters still make fake money the old-fashioned way—on printing presses. Here is the story of one of these professional counterfeiters.

1 Look at the boldfaced words and phrases in the reading and think about the questions.

1. Which words do you know the meaning of?

2. Can you use any of these words in a sentence?

2 Now read the story of Michael Landress, who was once a professional counterfeiter.

I MADE IT MYSELF

1   It took months of planning, of trying to find the perfect paper, of mixing and remixing ink to get the right color, of printing and reprinting to get the right feel, but I did it. I made a perfect copy of a $100 bill.

2   During the days, I did regular print jobs at the shop. Then every evening at five o'clock, I sent my workers home, hoping no one would ask why I stayed late. I pulled out the special paper, ink, and other equipment I hid away the night before and slowly, carefully, worked until the sun came up. I didn't have time to sleep. I was too **nervous** to sleep anyway. As I worked, I worried about the Secret Service[1] agents coming to get me. In the beginning, as I prepared the paper, I said to myself, "I'm just printing little blue and red hairlines on paper. They can't **arrest** me for that. I'm not **breaking the law**." Then as I printed the numbers, I said, "I'm just printing small numbers in four corners of a page. They can't arrest me for *this*. What I'm doing isn't illegal." Finally, as I got closer and closer to printing something they could arrest me for, I began to wonder, "Is this really that bad? Who am I hurting? I'm making myself a few thousand dollars so I can take my boy and move to Puerto Rico. I'm just trying to do my best for my family. Is that so wrong?"

3   After about three weeks of slow work, I finally printed out a whole sheet of $100 bills. I took out the magnifying glass and studied my work. "No. Oh, Ben, no. Ben, you don't look right," I said aloud to the empty shop. The portrait[2] of Ben Franklin on the front of the bill just didn't look right. To most people, he probably looked like the one on the real bill. However, I could see that it wasn't a perfect copy. I needed it to be perfect. So, slowly, painfully, I started over.

4   A week later, I was printing the last of the bills. I didn't hear them come in because of the noise of the press. I just looked up from studying the now-perfect portraits of Ben Franklin to see a gun at my head and hear the Secret Service agent say, "Just like getting caught with your hand in the cookie jar, huh, Mike?"

---

[1] **Secret Service:** government agency that tries to find and catch counterfeiters
[2] **portrait:** a drawing or painting of someone's head

COMPREHENSION

Answer the questions. Discuss your answers with a partner.

1. The title of the story is *I Made It Myself.* What does "It" refer to? _____

    _____

2. In Paragraph 3, Landress says, "No. Oh, Ben, no." Who is Ben? What was wrong? How does Michael feel? _____

3. In Paragraph 4, Landress says, "I didn't hear them come in because of the noise of the press." Who does "them" refer to? What were they coming to do? Why?_____

    _____

4. The story ends with "Just like getting caught with your hand in the cookie jar, huh, Mike?" What do you think "getting caught with your hand in the cookie jar" means?

    _____

■■■■■■■■■■■■■■■■■■■■■■■■■■■■■■■■ *GO TO* MyEnglishLab *FOR MORE VOCABULARY PRACTICE.*

READING SKILL

1 Read *I Made It Myself* again and think about how much time the story took. Underline the phrases in the story that help you know how much time each part of the story took.

UNDERSTANDING SEQUENCE OF EVENTS IN A STORY

When telling a story, a writer uses **time phrases** to show the passage of time between plot elements. Recognizing these time phrases helps readers understand the story's sequence of events.

Look at the examples and read the explanations:

- **"It took months** of planning. . . ."*(paragraph 1)*

This gives an overall time structure to the story.

- **"During the days**. . . ."*(paragraph 2)*

This shows that the paragraph describes actions that went on over a long period of time.

2 Work with a partner. Identify two additional time phrases and discuss how they move the story along.

1. Time phrase in paragraph 3: _____

    What does it tell us?

2. Time phrase in paragraph 4: _____

    What does it tell us?

■■■■■■■■■■■■■■■■■■■■■■■■■■■■■■■■■ *GO TO* MyEnglishLab *FOR MORE SKILL PRACTICE.*

STEP 1: Organize

There are two kinds of counterfeiters: casual counterfeiters, like the 14-year-old boy in Scottsdale, Arizona, and professional counterfeiters, like Mike Landress.

Based on Reading One (**R1**) and Reading Two (**R2**), compare the two kinds of counterfeiters. Look at the list of phrases. Then write each phrase in the correct box in the chart. Some phrases may be used twice.

- ~~artistic skills~~
- printing presses
- color-changing ink
- line doesn't change color with UV light
- a print shop
- special paper
- computer printer ink

- know how to run a printing press
- scanners
- microprint looks like black lines
- ink is not color-changing
- home computer skills
- computer printer paper
- no special line

	CASUAL COUNTERFEITERS (R1)	PROFESSIONAL COUNTERFEITERS (R2)
1. What kind of skills do they need?		*artistic skills*
2. What tools, equipment, and materials do they need?		
3. How can you tell their bills are fake?		

STEP 2: Synthesize

The U.S. government does a lot to prevent counterfeiting, but it has different ways of catching casual and professional counterfeiters.

Complete the two memos regarding counterfeit prevention. Use information from the chart in Step 1.

1.

U.S. Bureau of Counterfeit Prevention

To: Shopkeepers in the Washington, D.C. area

Re: Catching casual counterfeiters

We are finding many counterfeit bills in the Washington, D.C. area this month. These bills are made with home computer technology and are easy to recognize. Please help us to catch counterfeiters.

Tips for recognizing counterfeit bills:

1. (paper / feel) _____The paper feels different._____

2. (special line) _____

3. (microprint) _____

4. (your idea) _____

5. (your idea) _____

2.

U.S. Bureau of Counterfeit Prevention

To: All U.S. agents

Re: Professional counterfeiter investigation

Professionally-made counterfeit bills are showing up in the New York, Philadelphia, and Boston areas. We cannot rely on shopkeepers to help us find these counterfeiters because the bills are very well done and difficult to recognize as counterfeit.

Very few people have the equipment, materials, and skills to counterfeit this well. It is important that we find those people who have the special counterfeiting equipment and materials.

Here is a list of questions we need to answer in order to begin our investigation:

1. (printing presses) ___Who owns printing presses?_____

2. (ink) _____

3. (your idea) _____

4. (your idea) _____

GO TO MyEnglishLab TO CHECK WHAT YOU LEARNED.

VOCABULARY

REVIEW

1 The following sentences do not make sense. Cross out the boldfaced word or phrase. Above it, write the correct antonym (opposite) from the box so the sentence makes sense.

arrested	completely	illegal	prevent
breaking the law	~~counterfeiter~~	nervous	

1. When I got the $100 bill, I noticed that the paper didn't feel right. "Is it possible that a *counterfeiter* ~~government worker~~ made this?" I asked myself.

2. The police officer took the woman by the arms, put her in the police car, and took her to the police station. He **set** her **free.**

3. His legs were shaking. His heart was going very fast. His lips were dry. He felt very **relaxed** as he gave the bank the counterfeit money.

4. The fire destroyed everything in the shop. The expensive designer clothing and all the jewelry were **not at all** destroyed.

5. It's **not a problem** to make photocopies of money. Teachers should use real bills when they teach students about American money.

6. Take that dollar bill out of the copier! You are **following the law!**

7. New Zealand, Brazil, and China now use special plastic instead of paper for their bills to **make** counterfeiting **easier.**

2 Complete the sentences with the words from the box.

bill	equipment	fake	ink	scanner	technology

1. Printing presses, copiers, scanners, and magnifying glasses are different kinds of _____ used in counterfeiting.

2. Even new printing presses use _____ that is over 500 years old.

3. I want to be able to put this magazine photograph on my computer screen. I need a(n) _____.

4. Don't be fooled by that "Rolex" watch. It's cheap because it's _____.

5. I need change. Can I have four quarters for a one-dollar _____?

6. Professor Porter always corrected my papers with purple _____ since she didn't like red.

EXPAND

1 Money isn't the only counterfeit product. Look at the pictures of other counterfeit products. How can you tell that these products are fake? Discuss with a partner.

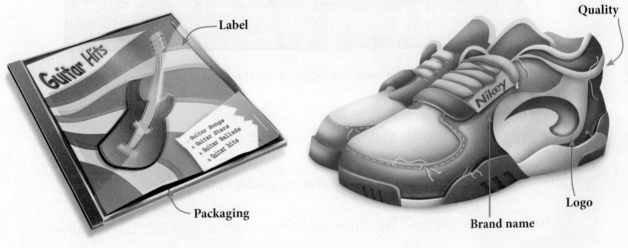

Label

Packaging

1. Pirated CD

Quality

Logo

Brand name

2. Imitation sports shoes

2 Read about Nicola and Jim, and look at the picture.

Nicola and Jim are at the flea market, a market where people sell lots of cheap products. Nicola is surprised that there are so many cheap designer products. Jim knows that these products are all fake.

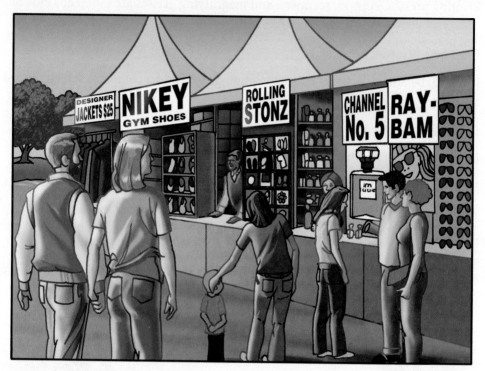

Now complete the conversation with the words from the box.

brand name	labels	packaging	quality
imitation	logo	pirated	

NICOLA: Jim! Look at this! They have Rayban sunglasses for only $25!

JIM: Nicola, those aren't real. Those are *Raybams*—the __brand name__ is spelled wrong!
1.

NICOLA: Oh. But what about these bottles of perfume? It's Chanel!

JIM: Can't you tell that those are fake? They have different _____ and
2.

_____.
3.

NICOLA: Oh, look! Here are some CDs of the Rolling Stones! I love the Rolling Stones!

JIM: These CDs are _____. Someone just copied the covers on their scanner.
4.

NICOLA: Well what about the shoes? These are Nikes, and they are really cheap!

JIM: You can tell that they are not Nikes because the _____ looks wrong . . .
5.
They are cheaper because the _____ is bad. They will probably fall apart in
6.
one week!

NICOLA: What about those jackets? They look like Hollister.

JIM: For $25? They are _____ Hollister. Nicola, *everything* here is fake!
7.

CREATE

Look at the picture and complete the conversation. Use as many of the words from the box as you can.

arrest	counterfeit	illegal	nervous	real
bills	counterfeiter	imitation	packaging	quality
brand name	equipment	label	~~pirated~~	scanner
completely	fake	logo	prevent	

NICOLA: Well, maybe *you* know that these products are all fake, but that kid over there is
buying a lot of stuff. Look! He just bought some software.

(continued on next page)

JIM: Oh, that is _____pirated_____. You can tell because _____.

NICOLA: And now he's buying _____.

How do you think he got all that money?

JIM: That's not real money. I think _____.

NICOLA: Really?_____.

JIM: It looks like he used _____.

NICOLA: You're right. He also seems _____.

JIM: Uh, oh. Look behind you! There are some policemen.

NICOLA: Do you think _____?

JIM: I don't know, but I think we should leave before there is trouble!

GO TO MyEnglishLab FOR MORE VOCABULARY PRACTICE.

GRAMMAR

1 Read the public service announcement. Underline the words that end in **-er**. Then answer the questions.

WARNING!
Counterfeit drugs can kill you!
Pharmacies are safer than Internet sites!

- Counterfeit drugs are more common today than 10 years ago. They are usually cheaper than real drugs, but they are very dangerous!

- These drugs are often for sale on the Internet. Buying things online is easier than going to a real pharmacy, but it can be dangerous.

- Always buy your medicines at pharmacies. If you want to check your drugs to see if they are real, ask your pharmacist to check. They can tell which pills are counterfeit and which are real.

---

1. What three words did you underline? _____

2. What word follows each of these words? _____

The words you underlined are **adjectives in the comparative form**.

COMPARATIVE FORM OF ADJECTIVES

1. Use the **comparative** form of adjectives to compare two people, places, or things.

   They are usually **cheaper** than real drugs.

   Buying things online is **easier** than going to the store.

2. If the adjective has one syllable, add *-er* to make the comparative.

   Add only *-r* if the word ends in *-e*.

fast	fast**er**
old	old**er**
large	larg**er**

3. When a one-syllable adjective ends in a consonant + vowel + consonant, double the last consonant and add *-er*.

big	big**ger**
hot	hot**ter**

4. If a two-syllable adjective ends in *-y*, change *y* to *i* and add *-er*.

easy	eas**ier**
busy	bus**ier**

5. Some adjectives have **irregular** comparative forms.

good	**better**
bad	**worse**

6. For most adjectives that have two or more syllables, add *more* before the adjective to make the comparative.

   Counterfeit drugs are **more common** today than 10 years ago.

7. Use *than* after the comparative form and before the second person, place, or thing.

   If the second person, place, or thing is understood, do not use *than*.

   This camera is **cheaper *than*** that one.

   This bag is **more expensive *than*** that one.

   Bart doesn't like his computer. He wants to buy one that is **faster**.

2 Read the following shoppers' blog on counterfeit merchandise. Complete the blog with the comparative form of the adjective in parentheses.

The Ultimate Shoppers' Blog

HOME

CONTACT

ABOUT US

You read it in the news every day. Police find millions of dollars in fake computers, clothing, drugs, and CDs every year. They say their job is

getting _____ because the copies get _____
           1. (hard)   2. (good)

each year. The copies are so good, it's difficult for even the police to know if

they are real or not. If the police can't tell, what is a shopper to do?

My advice:

Shop at a store you trust. Online you see some shampoo that is

_____ than what you pay at your salon. You could save $10
        3. (cheap)

per bottle. Who do you trust? Do you feel _____ trusting the
                                          4. (comfortable)

online company you don't know or the salon you visit every six weeks?

Know the price. Everyone wants to pay less. But you know a D&G

bag costs $1,500. When you see it for $100, don't buy it. Yes, the real

thing is _____. But it's real, not fake. Remember, it's
        5. (expensive)

_____ to tell the fakes from the real thing if you know
        6. (easy)

the price.

Be smart. Counterfeiters want you to believe them. But you have to be

_____ than them. Look at the label carefully. Pay attention to
        7. (smart)

the language. Look for mistakes in the label and in the tags.

3 Read the descriptions of two anti-counterfeit machines. Then write sentences comparing the two machines. Use the adjectives from the box.

Electronic Cash Scanner	Currency Validator Pen

$49.99	$12.98
Will last for 10 years TO USE: Place bills in machine and wait a few seconds for machine to electronically scan them.	Will test up to 5,000 bills TO USE: Make a small dot on each bill with the pen. Wait for the color to turn dark brown (counterfeit) or to turn yellow (good).
If bills are counterfeit, a red light flashes and an alarm sounds.	If bills are counterfeit, a dark brown spot appears on bill.

bad	difficult (to use)	expensive	good	slow
cheap	easy (to use)	fast	large	strong

1. _The electronic cash scanner is stronger than the currency validator pen._

2. _____

3. _____

4. _____

5. _____

6. _____

7. _____

8. _____

9. _____

10. _____

■ ■ ■ ■ ■ ■ ■ ■ ■ ■ ■ ■ ■ ■ GO TO MyEnglishLab *FOR MORE GRAMMAR PRACTICE AND TO CHECK WHAT YOU LEARNED.*

FINAL WRITING TASK

In this unit, you read about counterfeit money and counterfeit products like CDs, sports shoes, designer clothes, and watches.

Now you are going to **write a paragraph about a counterfeit product** of your choice. You are going to tell what the product is, where you can buy the product, and how you can tell it is fake. End your paragraph by saying if you think it's a good idea to buy this product. Use the vocabulary and grammar from the unit.*

PREPARE TO WRITE: Clustering

One way to get ideas for your paragraph about a counterfeit product is by **clustering**. Clustering helps you see your ideas and how they are connected. In a **cluster diagram**, the topic is in a large circle in the middle. New ideas are in smaller circles and are all connected to the topic.

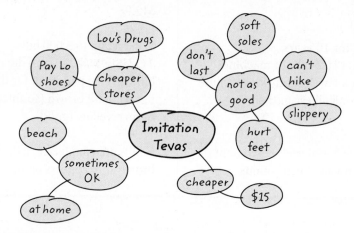

Make a cluster diagram for your product. Write the name of the product in the circle. Then link your ideas to the circle as you think of them.

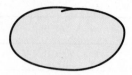

---

* For Alternative Writing Topics, see page 79. These topics can be used in place of the writing topic for this unit or as homework. The alternative topics relate to the theme of the unit but may not target the same grammar or rhetorical structures taught in the unit.

WRITE: A Well-organized Paragraph

To write a well-organized paragraph, you need to **select the right information**. Read the directions for your writing assignment carefully. They can often help you organize your ideas by telling you what information to include.

1 Go to page 74 and reread the directions for writing your paragraph about a fake product. Then read the list and check off the information you need to include. Cross out the things that you don't need to include in your paragraph.

_____ 1. ~~Describe counterfeit money.~~

_____ 2. Tell if you think it's a good idea to buy the product.

_____ 3. Tell exactly how much the counterfeit product costs.

_____ 4. Tell what the product is.

_____ 5. Tell about a time a store checked to see if the money you used was counterfeit.

_____ 6. Tell where to buy it.

_____ 7. Describe the people who make the product.

_____ 8. Describe how you can tell it is fake.

_____ 9. Tell how to find out if the fake product is legal or not.

_____ 10. List the ways the United States tries to prevent counterfeiting products.

2 Read the sentences about pirated software. They do not all belong in a paragraph for this assignment. Cross out the sentences that do not belong in this paragraph. Next to each sentence that remains, write a note telling what kind of information the sentence gives.

What the product is 1. Pirated software is one product that is counterfeit.

_____ 2. Pirated music CDs are also a big problem, especially for the musicians.

_____ 3. I can buy pirated software in some small computer stores I know.

_____ 4. You know it is pirated if it is very cheap.

(continued on next page)

_____ **5.** You can tell the software is pirated if the label is from a copy machine.

_____ **6.** Sometimes the seller gives you a CD that has no printing on it.

_____ **7.** Sometimes real copies of software cost more than a thousand dollars.

_____ **8.** I think it is wrong to buy pirated software because it is like stealing from the company.

3 Now list the information you need to include in your paragraph. Then write the first draft of your paragraph.

1. Tell what the product is: _____

2. Tell where to buy it: _____

3. Describe how you can tell it is fake: _____

4. Tell if you think buying the product is a good idea: _____

REVISE: Giving Explanations

Can a reader actually tell the difference between the fake product you describe and the real product? A reader often needs **more information**, **more detail**, and **more explanations**.

1 Read the paragraph about Keen sandals. The reader wanted more information to really help her tell the difference. Look at the questions she wrote.

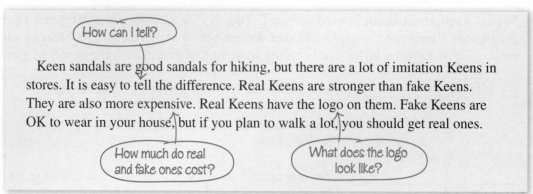

How can I tell?

Keen sandals are good sandals for hiking, but there are a lot of imitation Keens in stores. It is easy to tell the difference. Real Keens are stronger than fake Keens. They are also more expensive. Real Keens have the logo on them. Fake Keens are OK to wear in your house, but if you plan to walk a lot, you should get real ones.

How much do real and fake ones cost?

What does the logo look like?

Now the writer has rewritten the paragraph. See how much clearer it is.

Keen sandals are good sandals for hiking, but there are a lot of imitation Keens in stores. It is easy to tell the difference. Real Keens are stronger than fake Keens. If you pinch the soles with your fingers, Keens feel hard, but imitations feel very soft, like a pillow. Real Keens are also more expensive. They cost about $85, but you can get them on sale for $40 sometimes. If you are paying only $25 or less, the sandals are probably not real Keens. Real Keens have the logo on them. The logo is yellow letters on a black background. Fake Keens are OK to wear in your house, but if you plan to walk a lot, you should get real ones.

2 With a partner, read the following paragraph and write questions to show where you need more detail, just as the reader of the Keen paragraph did.

I like Obsession perfume by Calvin Klein, but I have to be careful to buy real Obsession and not fake. Guys sell fake Obsession perfume on the sidewalk in Los Angeles. The bottles are the same shape as real Obsession, but the label looks different. If you put the fake perfume on, it has the wrong smell. Fake Obsession is cheaper than real Obsession. But if you buy it, you waste your money because it smells very bad.

3 Share first drafts with a partner. Write questions on your partner's draft. The questions should help your partner give more information about how to tell the difference between the fake and the real product he or she describes.

4 Now look at your first draft and at your partner's questions. Give more information about how to tell the difference between the fake and the real product you describe.

■■■■■■■■■■■■■■■■■■■■■■■■■■■■■■■■■■■■■■ *GO TO* MyEnglishLab *FOR MORE SKILL PRACTICE.*

Go to MyEnglishLab and write the final draft of your paragraph. Carefully edit it for grammatical and mechanical errors, such as spelling, capitalization, and punctuation. Make sure you use some of the vocabulary and grammar from the unit. Use the checklist to help you write your final draft. Then submit your paragraph to your teacher.

FINAL DRAFT CHECKLIST

❑ Is your paragraph well organized? Does it have the right information?

❑ Does your paragraph tell about a counterfeit product?

❑ Does it tell where you can buy this counterfeit product?

❑ Does it explain how you can tell that this product is fake?

❑ Does it give your opinion about why it is or isn't a good idea to buy this product?

❑ Do you use comparative adjectives correctly?

❑ Do you use new vocabulary that you learned in this unit?

UNIT PROJECT

All countries work hard to prevent counterfeiting. Research ways that countries other than the United States do this. Decide which bills you think are most difficult to copy. Follow these steps:

STEP 1: Collect two or three bills from countries other than the United States. You might ask classmates from different countries or people who travel to lend you some bills.

STEP 2: Examine the bills carefully and take notes about what you notice. Pay attention to the features that might be difficult for a casual counterfeiter to copy. Here are some ways to examine the bills:

- Feel the paper. Does it feel special?

- Look at the bill. Use a magnifying glass, if you have one. Do you see any microprint or other fine details?

- Hold the bill up to a light (or a UV light if you have one). Do you see anything special?

- What else do you notice about the bill?

STEP 3: Look up the bills on the Internet. You can use search terms like: *security features on Chinese money*, or *counterfeit prevention in France*. Make notes about anything else you learn that each country does to prevent counterfeiting.

STEP 4: Set up a spreadsheet or a chart to organize your information.

WHAT MAKES BILLS DIFFICULT TO COPY?				
COUNTRY	FEATURES OF THE PAPER	FEATURES OF THE IMAGES	FEATURES YOU CAN ONLY SEE WITH STRONG OR UV LIGHT	OTHER FEATURES
1.				
2.				
3.				

STEP 5: Fill in your chart with the important information you learned.

STEP 6: Decide which bill you think is most difficult for a casual counterfeiter to copy and write a paragraph to tell your readers why you think so.

ALTERNATIVE WRITING TOPICS

Write about one of the topics. Use the vocabulary and grammar from the unit.

1. Write a paragraph comparing casual counterfeiters to professional counterfeiters. Use the information from the readings and from the exercises.

2. Suppose that you work in a store and that your boss asks you to choose an anti-counterfeiting tool for the store and to write her an email about it. You decide the store should buy the cash scanner.

   Look back at the exercise on page 73. Choose the reasons that best explain why you chose the scanner instead of the pen. Use these sentences to write your email.

3. The word *counterfeit* applies to anything fake. For example, you can buy counterfeit Levi's jeans, counterfeit music CDs, or counterfeit computer software.

   Making counterfeit computer software is a crime. People copy expensive software and then sell it for less than it costs in the stores.

   Write a paragraph comparing counterfeiting computer software to counterfeiting money. Which one is more difficult? Which is a more serious crime? Explain.

■■■■■■■■■■■■■■■■■■■■■■■ *GO TO* MyEnglishLab *TO WRITE ABOUT ONE OF THE ALTERNATIVE TOPICS, WATCH A VIDEO ABOUT MONEY, AND TAKE THE UNIT 3 ACHIEVEMENT TEST.* ■■■■■■■■■■■■■■■■■■■■■■■

SUBWAY
Etiquette

1 FOCUS ON THE TOPIC

1. What are the people in the photo doing?

2. Are any of them doing something they should not do? What are some examples of things that people shouldn't do in the subway?

3. What politeness rules do you think people should follow in the subway? Give one or two examples.

VOCABULARY

Inside a New York City subway car

Subway etiquette is the set of politeness rules for the people who ride (take) the subway. Other public transportation like buses or trains have similar rules. Some of these rules are written, like the ones shown by the signs above. But rules of etiquette are also often unwritten. Some examples of unwritten rules of etiquette in the New York subway are *Don't talk to people you don't know* and *Don't sit right next to passengers you don't know if there are other seats available.*

1 What do you do in the following situations? Take the quiz to see what kind of New York subway rider (passenger) you might be. Read each situation and circle your answer. Pay attention to the boldfaced words.

SUBWAY ETIQUETTE QUIZ

1. You are trying to enter the subway station, but your MetroCard[1] doesn't work.

   (A) You shout **rude** words and hit the turnstile[2] with your hand until a police officer comes to see what's going on.

   (B) You quickly try two more times, then ask a subway employee for help.

   (C) You try ten more times and say to the people waiting behind you: "You can never **rely on** these stupid machines! They are always broken!"

2. Your train arrives. As the doors open, you see that there are several people who want to get off the train.

   (A) You stand to the side so that you don't **block** the way.

   (B) You push through the doors as fast as you can to find a seat.

   (C) You stand in front of the door and let people go around you to get off.

3. An **elderly** woman gets on the train. She looks for a seat, but there are no more seats left. You have a seat.

   (A) You pretend to be asleep so that you don't **make eye contact with** her.

   (B) You stay where you are and tell her to hold on to the **pole** when the train starts moving.

   (C) You stand up and give your seat to the woman.

4. You have a cold and begin to **sneeze** on a crowded train. Someone hands you a tissue.[3]

   (A) You take it, say thank you, and blow your nose.

   (B) You pretend not to notice.

   (C) You ask, "Is there a 'no sneezing' rule? Is it your job to **enforce** it?"

---

[1] **MetroCard:** name of the card you need to have to ride the subway or the bus in New York City

[2] **turnstile:** a gate that spins around and only lets one person through at a time

[3] **tissue:** a paper handkerchief for wiping noses

Add up your points using this key.

1. Your score:	**2. Your score:**	**3. Your score:**	**4. Your score:**	**Your total score:**
A—0 points	**A**—2 points	**A**—1 point	**A**—2 points	_____
B—2 points	**B**—0 points	**B**—0 points	**B**—1 point	_____
C—1 point	**C**—1 point	**C**—2 points	**C**—0 points	_____

If your score is:

8 points: New York is proud to have you riding its subway. Thank you for being an excellent example of **civilized** behavior.

6–7 points: You have a few things to learn about how to behave in New York's subway. Watch other riders more carefully to learn about subway **etiquette**. And study the NYC Transit rules of conduct.

5 points or less: Please get a car. Or move to an island in the middle of the Arctic Ocean. Learn some **manners**.

2 Look back at the boldfaced words and phrases in the quiz. Then match the words and phrases on the left with the definitions on the right.

_j_ **1.** rude

_d_ **2.** rely on (something)

_f_ **3.** block

_g_ **4.** elderly

_h_ **5.** make eye contact with (someone)

_e_ **6.** pole

_b_ **7.** sneeze

_c_ **8.** manners

_a_ **9.** enforce (something)

_k_ **10.** civilized

_i_ **11.** etiquette

a. to make sure that people do something that they are supposed to do

b. to blow air through your nose suddenly (saying "Aaaaatchoo!")

c. polite ways of behaving (*That child has no _____!*)

d. to expect something to work right

e. a long round piece of metal for holding onto

f. to stand in the way

g. old

h. to look someone in the eyes

i. a set of politeness rules

j. not polite; hurtful

k. organized so that people are nice to each other and take care of each other

GO TO MyEnglishLab FOR MORE VOCABULARY PRACTICE.

PREVIEW

Editorials are articles in newspapers where writers give their opinions. The following editorial is from the City section of a New York newspaper.

Read the title and the first paragraph of the editorial. What do you think the writer's suggestion might be about? Check (✓) your answer.

_____ **1.** good places to visit on the subway

_____ **2.** the restaurants with the best service in New York

_____ **3.** how to make the subway nicer to ride

_____ **4.** how to get around New York without riding the subway

Now read the whole editorial.

A CIVILIZED SUGGESTION

By Dan Forman

1   There is a very long list of rules for the New York City subway. Don't put your feet on a seat, don't carry open cups of coffee or soda, don't take more than one seat, don't ride while drunk . . . Those are just a few of the rules. There are hundreds more.

2   With this many rules, why is it still so unpleasant to ride the subway?

3   Some people think that the problem is that no one **enforces** the rules. There aren't enough subway police, and the ones we have are too busy catching people who don't pay. Other passengers sometimes try to enforce rules. But you can't **rely on** them because New Yorkers have unwritten rules of **etiquette** against talking to strangers and **making eye contact with** strangers. How can you tell someone to take her shopping bags off the seat and throw away her Coke without talking to her or looking at her? It is difficult.

4   There are other New Yorkers who think that the subway is unpleasant because there are not *enough* rules. One rider wrote a letter to *The New York Times* a couple of weeks ago suggesting a few more subway rules. Here are some of the rules that she would like to see:

- Don't lean[1] on the **poles**. You prevent other people from holding on. They can fall down.
- Talk quietly. The trains are already too noisy.
- Cover your mouth and nose when you **sneeze** or cough. Other riders don't want to catch your cold.
- If your MetroCard doesn't work after three tries, ask a subway employee for help. Don't **block** the entrance.
- Give your seat to **elderly** passengers or to parents with small children.

5   Of course, anyone who knows the subway probably agrees that those are great ideas for rules. But polite people already do all of those things. If those unwritten rules of etiquette are written down, will the **rude** people be more likely to follow them? Will anyone enforce them? It doesn't make sense to make more rules that no one will enforce.

6   The real problem is that we are forgetting how to be nice to each other. It is embarrassing that we need a rule to tell us to give our seat to elderly passengers. Nobody should need to be reminded to do that.

7   I say we stop talking about the rules and try to remember our **manners**. Let's be nice to each other not because a police officer might tell us to get off the train, but because it is the right thing to do. *Then* New York City would be more **civilized**—both above ground and below.

---

[1] **lean:** to support yourself against a wall or other surface

MAIN IDEAS

1 Look again at the Preview on page 84. Was your prediction correct?

2 Check (✓) the statement that best describes the main idea of the editorial.

_✓_ **a.** The New York subway has plenty of rules, but police officers need to work harder to enforce them.

_____ **b.** People have lots of ideas about how to make the New York subway more pleasant to ride, but I think that we all need to just remember our manners.

_____ **c.** Elderly passengers often have to stand up on the New York subway. All passengers need to work to enforce the etiquette rules about this.

_____ **d.** New York has many etiquette rules, such as *Don't make eye contact* and *Don't talk to people you don't know.*

DETAILS

Circle the best ending for each statement.

1. The New York subway has _a_ .

   a. a long list of rules

   b. only a few very important rules

   c. no rules

2. The writer thinks that riding the New York City subway is _b_ .

   a. always a good experience

   b. very difficult

   c. not pleasant

3. Some people think that _b_ should enforce the rules more.

   a. strangers

   b. police and other passengers

   c. passengers who take more than one seat

4. *Don't make eye contact* and *Don't talk to strangers* are examples of _a_ .

   a. general etiquette in New York City

   b. rules that one rider would like to have on the subway

   c. New York subway rules

5. *Don't lean on the poles* and *Talk quietly* are examples of _____

    a. new subway rules that one rider suggested

    b. New York subway rules

    c. rules that the author wants to see

MAKE INFERENCES

INFERRING THE AUTHOR'S ATTITUDE

Authors give clear opinions in editorials. For example, Dan Forman's opinion is at the end of the editorial, in paragraphs 6 and 7:

- "The real problem is that we are forgetting how to be nice to each other. . . . I say we stop talking about the rules and try to remember our manners."

Readers can **infer** (guess) even more about the author's attitude (beliefs) by reading details in the editorial carefully.

Look at the example and read the explanation.

- True or False?

    _____ Dan Forman thinks we need more enforcement of the rules.
    (The answer is False.)

In paragraph 3, the author tells us: "Some people think that the problem is that no one enforces the rules." *(Notice he says "Some people . . .", not "we" or "I".)*

In paragraph 7, the author tells us: "Let's be nice to each other not because a police officer might tell us to get off the train, but because it is the right thing to do." *(Police officers should not be the reason we are nice to each other.)*

After reading the text closely, we can **infer** that the statement is false. Dan Forman probably does not agree that we need more enforcement of the rules.

Which opinions does Dan Forman agree with? Refer to the paragraphs in parentheses, and write **T** (true) or **F** (false) next to each statement.

Dan Forman agrees . . .

_____ **1.** we should tell strangers what to do. *(paragraph 3)*

_____ **2.** we need *more* rules. *(paragraph 5)*

_____ **3.** we should remember how to be nice to each other. *(paragraph 6)*

Now discuss your answers with a partner. Point out in each paragraph the sentences, words, or phrases that helped you find the answers.

EXPRESS OPINIONS

Discuss the questions with a partner. Give your opinions. Then share your answers with the class.

1. After reading "A Civilized Suggestion," do you think that New York's subway is less pleasant than the subway or bus in other cities? What makes you think so?

2. Which of Dan Forman's opinions do you agree with? Why?

■■■■■■■■■■■■■■■■■■■■■■■■■■■■■ *GO TO* MyEnglishLab *TO GIVE YOUR OPINION ABOUT ANOTHER QUESTION.*

READING TWO | RIDING THE SUBWAY IN JAPAN

READ

1 Look at the boldfaced words and phrases in the reading and think about the questions.

1. Which words do you know the meaning of?

2. Can you use any of these words in a sentence?

2 Now read this blog from a San Francisco woman about subway etiquette in Tokyo.

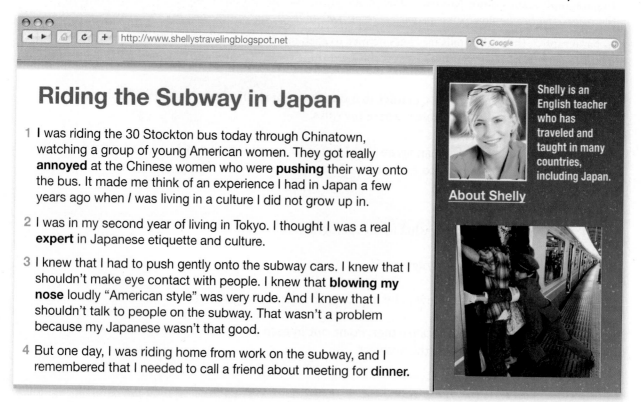

http://www.shellystravelingblogspot.net

Riding the Subway in Japan

Shelly is an English teacher who has traveled and taught in many countries, including Japan.

About Shelly

1 I was riding the 30 Stockton bus today through Chinatown, watching a group of young American women. They got really **annoyed** at the Chinese women who were **pushing** their way onto the bus. It made me think of an experience I had in Japan a few years ago when *I* was living in a culture I did not grow up in.

2 I was in my second year of living in Tokyo. I thought I was a real **expert** in Japanese etiquette and culture.

3 I knew that I had to push gently onto the subway cars. I knew that I shouldn't make eye contact with people. I knew that **blowing my nose** loudly "American style" was very rude. And I knew that I shouldn't talk to people on the subway. That wasn't a problem because my Japanese wasn't that good.

4 But one day, I was riding home from work on the subway, and I remembered that I needed to call a friend about meeting for **dinner**.

I took out my cell phone and called her. Of course, if you know the Tokyo subway, you know that there are "no cell phones" signs everywhere. But I also noticed that many passengers used their phones on the subway. I thought that the no cell phones rule in Japan was like the no food rule on the New York City subway. It's a rule, but no one follows it, and no one enforces it.

5 As I was talking, other passengers looked at me sideways like Japanese people do when they think you are being rude. One elderly woman shook her head and looked straight at me.

6 I finished my conversation, and I got off the train. I was very **confused**. Japanese people use their phones. Why can't I do the same? I asked myself.

7 Later that evening, I told my friend about the experience. She smiled. "The rule is *no talking* on cell phones," she said. "The others are all text messaging[1] or playing games on their phones. Sometimes they check their voicemail. Occasionally they whisper[2] a very short message to someone on a cell phone. But they never have whole conversations on their phones in the subway."

8 I was embarrassed.[3] I still had a lot to learn. Even though I knew a lot of Japanese habits, I was still American.

社でやろう。
Please do it at the office.

---

[1] **text messaging:** sending a written message on a cell phone
[2] **whisper:** speak very quietly
[3] **embarrassed:** feeling ashamed; feeling like you did something stupid

COMPREHENSION

Circle the best answer to complete each statement.

1. The writer ___b___ in Japan.

   a. went on vacation

   b. lived

2. The writer thought that she understood _____.

   a. Japanese subway etiquette

   b. the Tokyo subway system

3. One thing that she did not understand was _____.

   a. how to use her cell phone

   b. when it is OK to use a cell phone on the subway

(continued on next page)

4. The other passengers looked at her when she ____.

    a. had a conversation on her cell phone

    b. tried to speak Japanese

5. When Japanese people use their cell phones on the subway, they are ____.

    a. having long conversations with their friends

    b. text messaging or playing games

GO TO MyEnglishLab FOR MORE VOCABULARY PRACTICE.

READING SKILL

1 Read Reading Two again. Answer the questions.

1. What part of the story is the most exciting? _____

_____

2. When did the people in the story feel most anxious or worried? _____

_____

3. How did the story end? _____

IDENTIFYING THE MAIN ELEMENTS OF A STORY

Stories usually have these four main elements:

1. Important **background information** about the main character(s),

2. A conflict: two characters or two elements that don't understand or agree with each other.

3. A climax: a high point of the story when the elements in conflict crash together. The climax is usually the most exciting point in the story.

4. A resolution: something makes the conflict go away, or become weaker.

If you know these elements, you can understand the story quickly.

IMPORTANT BACKGROUND INFORMATION	MAIN CONFLICT	CLIMAX	RESOLUTION
Shelly is an American. She lives in Tokyo.	Shelly and Japanese culture.	Shelly uses her phone on the subway and several passengers make her uncomfortable.	Shelly learns that Japanese people think it is rude to have a conversation on a cell phone in the subway.

2 Work with a partner. Read the paragraph about another experience with public transportation, and fill in the story chart below.

The English are famous for standing in line for everything. But I didn't know that in 1993 when I went there. I am from Senegal. I studied English for many years, and one summer I got a scholarship to study in England. I arrived at Heathrow airport and found my bus stop to go to my dormitory in London. The bus came, and I gave my suitcase to the helper. Then I started to get on the bus. But an Englishwoman next to me yelled at me. "Young man! What do you think you are doing?!" She looked at me angrily. I heard her friend say, "Some people are so rude!" She was looking at me, too. I wanted to cry! I was excited to be in England, but these English people were already so angry at me, and I did not understand why. Luckily, another African man close by understood my problem. He tapped my shoulder and pointed at the line. "Brother, you need to stand in the line," he said. I looked behind me and saw 15 people in line. The African man smiled and said, "It's OK. You'll learn. The English stand in line for everything." I was very embarrassed, but at least I understood.

IMPORTANT BACKGROUND INFORMATION	MAIN CONFLICT	CLIMAX	RESOLUTION
He is from Senegal. he studied English for many years, and one summer he got a scholarship in England	He England, h has to stand in the line for everything thing	Englishwomen Gre so rude	He learns that he has to stand in the line.

GO TO MyEnglishLab FOR MORE SKILL PRACTICE.

STEP 1: Organize

Read the list of etiquette rules (written and unwritten) mentioned in Reading One (**R1**) and Reading Two (**R2**). Which rules are for the New York City subway, and which are for the Tokyo subway? Which rules are for both New York City and Tokyo? Check (✓) the correct column(s).

SUBWAY ETIQUETTE RULES	NYC SUBWAY (R1)	TOKYO SUBWAY (R2)
1. Don't put your feet on a seat.	✓	✓
2. Don't carry open cups of coffee or soda.	✓	✓
3. Push gently when getting on crowded subway cars.		✓
4. Don't ride while drunk.		
5. Don't make eye contact with strangers.		
6. Talk quietly.		
7. Don't take more than one seat.	✓	✓
8. Don't talk to strangers.		
9. Don't blow your nose loudly.		
10. Don't talk on your cell phone.		✓

STEP 2: Synthesize

Complete the conversation between Shelly, the blogger from Reading Two, and her friend Rachel. Use information from the chart in Step 1.

Rachel January 24, 2013 4:08 PM

Thanks so much for your posting about riding the Japanese subway! I just got a job in Tokyo, so I will be there soon. From your blog, I understand that there are a few subway etiquette rules that are different over there. For example,

You shouldn't make eye contact with people, you can't use cellphones in the subway. etc.

Is there anything else I should know?

You don't say anything about the pushers. I have seen photos of those guys who push you onto the trains! I am worried about that! Let me know if you have any more advice!

Shelly January 25, 2013 6:20 AM

Don't worry about the pushers. They are only at a few stations and only at the busiest times.

Most of the other subway rules are the same as here in New York.

For example, _don't ride when you're drunk. etc_

Send me an email when you get to Tokyo! I would love to stay in touch!

Rachel January 25, 2013 11:20 AM

Thanks! That would be great! I will contact you. I am sure I will need more advice.

Enter your comment...

3 FOCUS ON WRITING

VOCABULARY

REVIEW

Read "An Open Letter to Subway Riders." Decide what kind of word (noun, adjective, or verb) you need to fill each blank. Look at the lists in the box. Choose the correct word from the appropriate list and write it in the blank.

Nouns	Adjectives	Verbs
etiquette	annoyed	blocking
expert	civilized	blow his nose
eye contact	confused	enforce
manners	elderly	push
pole	~~rude~~	rely on
		sneeze

An Open Letter to New York Subway Riders

Being a New York subway rider like you, I know that in our subway it is _____rude_____
1.

to talk to strangers, and I also know that we should not make _____eyecontact_____ with
2.

each other.

I am no _____expert_____ on subway rules, but I do know about being polite. And I think
3.

we, New York subway riders, are forgetting some basic rules of _____etiquette_____.
4.

Yesterday, I was on the A train when a very _____elderly_____ man got on the train. As the
5.

train started to go, the poor man had to hold on to a _____pole_____ so that he didn't fall
6.

down. There were young people sitting in the seats around him. I was so _____
7.

with them! None of them moved. There was no one to _____ the "give your
8.

seat to elderly passengers" rule, so I stood up. I was far from the old man, so I called to him,

and he started to come my way. He certainly wanted a seat. But there was a woman who was

_____ the way. So the poor man had to stand there. He was too polite to
       9.

_____ her out of the way. To make things worse, there was a kid next to him who
     10.

seemed to have a terrible cold. He started to _____ on the old man. I wanted to
                                         11.

hand that kid a tissue for him to _____, but I didn't.
                   12.

I thought that New York was a _____ city, but I guess I was
                   13.

_____. You can't _____ anyone here to have good
    14.   15.

_____ anymore.
    16.

EXPAND

What is the correct response to each of the statements? Pay attention to the boldfaced words. Match each statement with a response from the list on the next page. Each response can be used more than once.

Statements

_a_ **1.** I gave my seat to a woman with three small children yesterday. It felt like the **polite** thing to do.

_d_ **2.** My newspaper blew out of my hands when the train came. I didn't want to **litter**, but I couldn't pick the paper up off the tracks.

_b_ **3.** I did not have a MetroCard, and I didn't have time to **wait my turn** at the MetroCard machine, so I just jumped over the turnstile.

_d_ **4.** I know that it is **impolite** to talk on a cell phone on the bus. But I just found out that my father was in the hospital.

_c_ ~~b~~ **5.** Where I come from, it's polite to say hello to other people on a long bus ride. So I **greeted** everyone when I got on the bus to Chicago.

_d_ **6.** I felt bad that I didn't **tip** the taxi driver. But my wallet was stolen earlier today, and I only had enough money for the taxi ride.

_a_ **7. I stood in line** to wait for the train in London since that was what everyone else seemed to be doing.

(continued on next page)

Responses

a. Good, you **followed the rules**. That was the right thing to do.

b. You **broke the rules**. You shouldn't do that.

c. What you did is **against the rules** of etiquette in the United States. These are unwritten rules, but they are still rules that you should learn.

d. Well, that's an **exception to the rule**. In unusual situations it is OK not to follow the rules.

CREATE

Read the letters to an advice column about public transportation etiquette. Write a response to each letter. Try to use the words in parentheses for each one.

1.

> I am always annoyed when I take a taxi and I pay the driver, and he asks if I want change. Is that rude or am I crazy?
>
> —John, Chicago

Dear John: (against the rules of etiquette / tip)

Asking "Do you want change?" is not against the rules of etiquette. The driver is trying to save you time. You can simply say "Yes, I want change" and then decide how much money you want to tip the driver.

2.

> I take the train to work every morning. I always listen to music or the radio with my earbuds. My boyfriend thinks I am rude because I can't hear people talk to me when I have earbuds in. But I don't really want to talk to people early in the morning. What do you think?
>
> —Michelle, Washington D.C.

Dear Michelle: (follow the rules / impolite)

_____

_____

_____

3.

I just arrived here in New York from Togo, West Africa, to study for a year. I ride buses everywhere. But sometimes I get a little lost. I am afraid to ask the bus drivers for help because there are big signs on all the buses that say *Do not talk to the driver*. I am afraid to even say hello to the driver. How can I ask if I am on the right bus without breaking the rules?

—Aliou, New York City

Dear Aliou: (manners / greet / exception)

_____

_____

_____

GO TO MyEnglishLab FOR MORE VOCABULARY PRACTICE.

GRAMMAR

1 Underline the verbs in the list of suggestions from Readings One and Two. Then answer the questions.

- Don't lean on the poles.
- Talk quietly.
- Cover your mouth and nose when you sneeze or cough.
- Don't block the entrance.
- Give your seat to elderly passengers or to parents with small children.
- Please don't talk on your cell phone.

1. Is there a subject in any of the sentences above?

2. Who is expected to do the things listed above?

IMPERATIVE SENTENCES

1. Use the imperative when you want to give clear **directions** or **orders**.	**Cover** your mouth and nose. **Talk** quietly. **Don't block** the entrance.
2. To form the imperative, use the **base form** of the verb.	**Take** your feet off the seat. **Push** gently.
3. In the negative, use *don't* before the base form of the verb.	*Don't* **lean** on the pole.
4. The subject of an imperative sentence is always *you*. We never state the subject unless we are addressing someone in particular.	CORRECT: **Talk** quietly. INCORRECT: **You talk** quietly. **Mario**, talk quietly.
5. To make a polite request, use the imperative with *please* at either the beginning or end of the sentence. If *please* is at the end of the sentence, there is a comma before it.	*Please* don't talk on your cell phone. Be quiet, *please*. Don't push, *please*.

2 Make imperative statements. Use the correct form of the verbs in parentheses.

1. ___Don't smoke___ on airplanes.
   (smoke / not)

2. ___Please turn off___ your cell phone at the movies.
   (turn off)

3. ___Don't look at___ your iPod in class, please.
   (look at / not)

4. ___Don't sing___ at a concert.
   (sing / not)

5. ___Don't park___ in a red zone.
   (park / not)

6. ___Please, tip___ your taxi driver at least 10 percent.
   (tip)

7. ___please, take out___ your earbuds when you talk to me!
   (take out)

3 Rewrite the rules or suggestions for polite behavior, using the imperative. Remember that you can use "please."

1. People shouldn't play loud music on the bus.

   _____

2. There is no smoking on the bus.

   _____

3. You should always say hello to your driver.

   _____

4. Shawn, you know that it's against the rules to talk to the driver.

   _____

5. Making eye contact with strangers is against New York's rules of etiquette.

   _____

■■■■■■■■■■■ *GO TO* MyEnglishLab *FOR MORE GRAMMAR PRACTICE AND TO CHECK WHAT YOU LEARNED.*

FINAL WRITING TASK

In this unit, you read about subway etiquette in New York and Tokyo. Now think about a city you know well. What kind of etiquette does it have on its public transportation (subway, buses, taxis, trains, etc.)?

You are going to *write a Web page about etiquette on a type of transportation* in that city. First, you will give some information about the type of transportation you chose. Then you will give a list of important rules of etiquette for this type of transportation. Use the vocabulary and grammar from the unit.*

PREPARE TO WRITE: Listing

Listing is making a list of your ideas before you begin to write. When you make a list, it is not necessary to write complete sentences.

1 Choose a type of public transportation that you know well. Fill in the city or town and type of transportation you are writing about. List all of the rules that you can think of.

City or Town: _Japan_

Type of Transportation: _Taxi_

Rules of Etiquette:
1. No smoking
2. Don't ride when you are drunk
3. Don't open or close the door.
4. Don't make eye contact
5. Don't talk with driver
6. Don't play loud music in the taxi
7. Don't give tip

---

* For Alternative Writing Topics, see page 105. These topics can be used in place of the writing topic for this unit or as homework. The alternative topics relate to the theme of the unit but may not target the same grammar or rhetorical structures taught in the unit.

2   Look at your list and cross out the rules that are less important. Keep the rules that are the most important. You should list about five rules.

WRITE: A Web Page

WRITING TO GIVE GENERAL INFORMATION

A **Web page** is a place on the Internet that gives information about a particular subject. So, writing a Web page is writing to inform. When you write to inform people about something, you often write in the **"second person"** (using *you*, not *I*). This is not the place to tell your own stories. You should include only general information about the subject you are writing about.

1   Look at the two introductions to a Web page about the Seattle streetcars. Check (✓) the one that gives you the clearest information about streetcars in Seattle.

○ **A.**

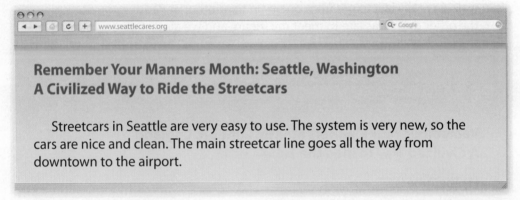

○ **B.**

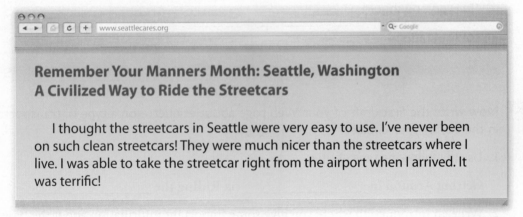

2 Look at this introduction to a Web page about the London Underground (familiarly called the Tube). Rewrite each sentence so that it is not about the writer.

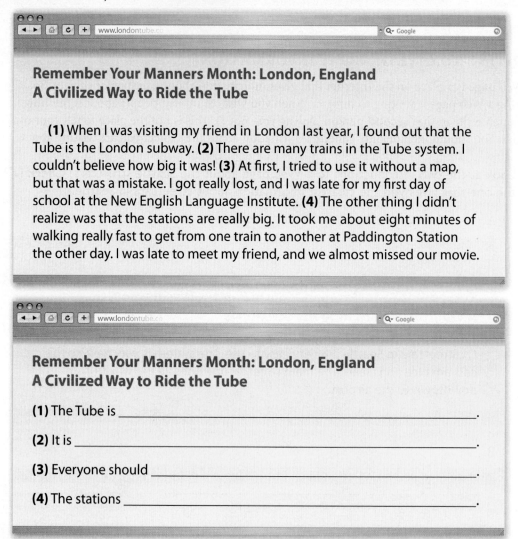

Remember Your Manners Month: London, England
A Civilized Way to Ride the Tube

(1) When I was visiting my friend in London last year, I found out that the Tube is the London subway. **(2)** There are many trains in the Tube system. I couldn't believe how big it was! **(3)** At first, I tried to use it without a map, but that was a mistake. I got really lost, and I was late for my first day of school at the New English Language Institute. **(4)** The other thing I didn't realize was that the stations are really big. It took me about eight minutes of walking really fast to get from one train to another at Paddington Station the other day. I was late to meet my friend, and we almost missed our movie.

Remember Your Manners Month: London, England
A Civilized Way to Ride the Tube

(1) The Tube is _____.

(2) It is _____.

(3) Everyone should _____.

(4) The stations _____.

3 Now write the first draft of your Web page about etiquette on a type of transportation in the city of your choice.

1. Use the following type of title:

Getting Around in _____ OR **Riding the _____**

2. Write an introduction where you give some important information about the type of transportation that you are writing about.

3. List a few rules (written or unwritten) that riders should know about.

REVISE: Using Parallel Structure

When you write a list, it is a good idea to make all the items in the list **parallel**. Each item should start with the same **grammatical structure** (noun, verb form, gerund, etc.). This makes them clearer and easier to read. Lists that use different grammatical structures at the beginning of each item can be difficult to read.

1 Underline the verb forms in each list. Which list is clearer? Check (✓) **A** or **B**.

○ **A.**

A few rules of etiquette for riding the Tube are:

- Walk quickly in the stations.
- Don't eat on the trains.
- Study your map before you begin your trip (so that you don't have to stop and block the way in the station).

○ **B.**

There are several rules for riding the Seattle streetcars:

- Eating is against the rules.
- You should buy a ticket before you get on the train.
- You have to put your bicycle in the end of the car where it says "Bikes."
- Don't smoke.

2 Rewrite the list of rules for the Seattle streetcars, using parallel structure.

There are several rules for riding the Seattle streetcars:

- _____
- _____
- _____
- _____

3 Now go back to the first draft of your Web page. Look at your list of rules and underline the verb forms in each rule. If there are rules that are not parallel, correct them so that they all start with the same grammatical structure.

■■■■■■■■■■■■■■■■■■■■■■■■■■■■■■■■■■■■■ *GO TO* MyEnglishLab *FOR MORE SKILL PRACTICE.*

Go to MyEnglishLab and write the final draft of your Web page. Carefully edit it for grammatical and mechanical errors, such as spelling, capitalization, and punctuation. Make sure you use some of the vocabulary and grammar from the unit. Use the checklist to help you write your final draft. Then submit your Web page to your teacher.

FINAL DRAFT CHECKLIST

❑ Does the title of your Web page tell where and what kind of transportation you are writing about?

❑ Does it give general information about this kind of transportation?

❑ Does it avoid stories from your own personal experience?

❑ Does it give information that would be useful to a reader who is going to visit this city and take this type of transportation?

❑ Does your Web page tell about rules for riding this type of public transportation?

❑ Do the rules in the list all follow parallel structure?

❑ Do you use the imperative correctly?

❑ Do you use new vocabulary that you learned in this unit?

UNIT PROJECT

Work with a partner. Choose a place that you both want to travel to and that you don't know very well. Research this culture's rules of etiquette. Follow these steps:

STEP 1: Choose the place that you would like to go to.

STEP 2: Divide your work so that each of you researches different categories of etiquette. Some of the categories you might research are:

- eating
- traveling
- doing business
- dating
- being a university student
- meeting new people

STEP 3: Interview people in your class to see if anyone knows anything about this place. You might ask the following question:

What rules of etiquette for (eating) are different from here?

STEP 4: Search on the Internet about "etiquette in _____." You will find a lot of information. Try to find the etiquette rules that are mentioned several times in several websites.

STEP 5: Make a list of the rules that you need to remember if you go to this country. You might want to list them by category.

STEP 6: Share your results with the class.

ALTERNATIVE WRITING TOPICS

Write about one of the topics. Use the vocabulary and grammar from the unit.

1. Your newspaper is asking for suggestions for new rules for the public transportation system in your town. Write an email giving your suggestions for rules you would like to see. Be sure to explain what type of public transportation you are writing about.

2. Sometimes people from one culture think that people from another culture are rude. In reality, they are just following different rules of etiquette. Write two paragraphs comparing etiquette in two cultures you know that are very different. What rules might help people in those two cultures get along?

■■■■■■■■■■■■■■■■■■■■■■■■ *GO TO* MyEnglishLab *TO WRITE ABOUT ONE OF THE ALTERNATIVE TOPICS,*
WATCH A VIDEO ABOUT ETIQUETTE, AND TAKE THE UNIT 4 ACHIEVEMENT TEST. ■■■■■■■■■■■■■■■■■■■■

WE ARE WHAT WE Eat

1 FOCUS ON THE TOPIC

1. What kind of food can you buy in this store?

2. What information can you find on the signs?

3. How do you choose your food?

GO TO MyEnglishLab TO CHECK WHAT YOU KNOW.

VOCABULARY

1 Read the post by a farmer in Vermont who writes a weekly blog for his customers. Try to understand the boldfaced words without looking them up in a dictionary.

Farm News

May 15, 2013

Hello everyone. Thomas O'Neill here again. It's a difficult year for farming. Last month, I wrote about the weather problems. Last week, I told you about the annoying **weeds** that grow everywhere. This week's problem starts with the **insects**. You name them, we have them. They eat the leaves and the fruit of many of my plants.

Wheat field

You all know that I grow wheat and other **grains**, right? Well, last year, insects ate half of my wheat. It's a big problem. This year, Wallace Simpson, one of my workers, wants to kill them with "Insect-Be-Gone." I am not going to **approve** "Insect-Be-Gone" to be used on my farm. I don't like to use any chemicals. I'm afraid that if the insects all die, the birds (that eat the insects) might not have enough food. If the bird **population** goes down, animals that eat the birds will have problems. Killing all the insects might break the **food chain**. One little change (killing all the wheat-eating insects) could create other larger changes down the chain.

Some of my neighbors are excited about a new GMO[1] wheat that scientists just created. It has extra vitamins, and insects won't eat it. It's a special kind of wheat that **resists** the insects. I understand the **benefits** of this wheat, but I'm worried about the problems it might cause. Nature is very **complex**. If you change something here, many things may change there. I am definitely not going to try the GMO wheat.

---

[1] **GMO: genetically modified organism,** a plant or animal made by scientists for a special purpose

I know. I know. I won't use chemicals or GMO wheat. Simpson thinks I'm old-fashioned. But I tell him, "Simpson, farmers need to take care of the **environment**. If you use things that are not natural on the farm, there will be problems with the animals, plants, and water all around us."

I might just have to be OK with the insects getting half my wheat.

—Posted by O'Neill at 7:58 A.M.

2 Match the words on the left with the definitions on the right.

_h_ 1. resist

_____ 2. weed

_____ 3. benefit

_____ 4. complex

_____ 5. insect

_____ 6. population

_____ 7. environment

_____ 8. approve

_____ 9. food chain

_____ 10. grain

a. to say it is OK; to allow people to do it

b. very small animal, for example an ant or a bee

c. not simple

d. positive result

e. natural world; area around us

f. group of plants and animals that rely on each other for food; for example, large birds eat snakes, snakes eat rabbits, rabbits eat grass

g. plant grown for food, for example, rice, wheat and barley

h. to fight against; to not get harmed by

i. the number of members of a group

j. wild plant that people don't want in their farms or gardens

••• *GO TO* MyEnglishLab *FOR MORE VOCABULARY PRACTICE.*

Read the title of the article and look at the photos. How can a fish be "new"? Why is it different from other fish? Check (✓) three statements that you think are true about the "new fish" in the article.

_____ **a.** It eats more than other fish.

_____ **b.** It grows faster than other fish.

_____ **c.** It is made by scientists.

_____ **d.** It was just discovered.

_____ **e.** It tastes better than other fish.

Now read the article.

A NEW FISH IN TOWN

Atlantic salmon swimming upstream

1 A new kind of salmon might arrive at your market soon. Why is this fish special? AquAdvantage salmon grows twice as fast as other salmon because it is a GMO, or a genetically modified organism.

2 GMOs are plants or animals that contain DNA[1] from other types of plants or animals. Scientists put DNA from two other types of fish into the DNA of a regular salmon. The result is an AquAdvantage salmon that becomes full-grown in 18 months, instead of three years. AquAdvantage salmon tastes and looks just like regular salmon. For salmon farmers, the **benefits** are clear: They can sell their fish more quickly. And for a hungry world **population**, more salmon means cheaper salmon and better health for many people.

3 If the U.S. government **approves** AquAdvantage salmon, it will be the first GMO fish in U.S. supermarkets. But Americans have been eating GMO vegetables and

Scientist examining DNA model

---

[1]**DNA:** genes in all living things

grains for almost 20 years. Around 85% of the corn, and 93% of soybeans[2] in the United States are GMO. Corn and soybeans are very important in the U.S. for both animals and people. Lots of food like cereal, crackers, and chips contain corn and soy.

4 Each GMO is created for a different reason. Some GMOs **resist insects** or dry weather; some last longer in supermarkets; some have more vitamins; still others, like the salmon, grow faster.

5 But not everyone is happy about GMO foods. Many countries, such as Peru, Ireland, Japan, Egypt, and Switzerland do not allow farmers to grow GMOs at all. Other countries including Australia, New Zealand, China, Saudi Arabia, Thailand, India, Chile, and South Africa require "contains GMO" labels for these foods. These countries worry that GMOs are bad for people's health and for the **environment**.

6 Although GMOs are very common in the U.S., many people think that they create more problems than they solve. GMO

GMO corn in the United States

---

[2]**soybeans:** beans that are used to make tofu
[3]**herbicides:** chemicals that kill plants

corn is an example of a GMO that solved one problem but is creating two more. To understand this example, one needs to know a little bit about GMO corn and farming: Most corn farmers use herbicides[3] to kill **weeds**. GMO corn resists herbicides. Before GMO corn, farmers could only use a little bit of herbicide because too much killed the corn, too. With GMO corn, farmers can use more herbicides, and this makes it easier to kill the weeds. It is clear why farmers thought GMO corn was such a good idea in 1990 when the U.S. government approved it. Farmers were able to grow more corn with less work.

7 But because farmers are using more herbicides in GMO corn-growing areas, today we see two new problems. The first

A butterfly feeding on a flower

problem is that butterflies are disappearing. The butterfly population is 80% lower in these areas than it was 20 years ago. Herbicides kill a wild plant called milkweed, and butterflies need milkweed to live. So the GMO corn is changing the whole **food chain** in these areas. The second problem in GMO corn-growing areas is that many weeds now resist herbicides. Weeds that herbicides cannot kill are called superweeds. Before GMO corn, there was

(continued on next page)

one superweed. Now there are 22, so corn farmers have new problems to face. This example shows how **complex** the benefits and problems of GMOs can be.

8　The AquAdvantage company tells us that the new fish will not create any problems for the environment. But can we believe them? Monsanto, the company that created GMO corn, did not predict any problems from GMO corn 20 years ago either. The world's population is almost ten billion, and those people need to eat. Will GMO foods like AquAdvantage salmon help us feed the world? Or will they create more problems than they solve?

MAIN IDEAS

1　Look again at the Preview on page 110. How did your predictions help you understand the article?

2　Each statement tells the main idea of a paragraph in "A New Fish in Town." Read a statement, then write the correct paragraph number next to it.

Paragraph

a. Rules about GMOs are different in different countries. 5

b. GMO salmon might be available soon in the United States. 1

c. Americans have been eating GMO vegetables and grains for a long time. 3

d. GMOs can solve a lot of problems, but we don't know if they will create more problems in the future. 8

e. GMO corn has created two problems for the environment. 7

f. GMOs are created to solve many different problems. 2

g. GMOs contain DNA from other species. They have many benefits. 4

h. GMO corn is an example of a GMO with both benefits and problems. 6

3　Check (✓) the statement that best describes the main idea of the whole article.

_____ a. AquAdvantage salmon might solve many of the world's problems.

_____ b. Most of the world does not allow GMOs, but the United States allows many GMO fruits, vegetables, grains, and now meats.

_____ c. GMOs, including the new AquAdvantage salmon, have a lot of benefits, but they also create problems that we cannot predict.

DETAILS

Read each statement. Decide if it is true or false. Write **T** (*true*) or **F** (*false*) next to it.
Compare your answers with a partner's.

___T___ **1.** It is now illegal to farm, sell, and eat the GMO AquAdvantage salmon in the
United States.

___T___ **2.** GMO salmon grows much faster than regular salmon.

___F___ **3.** AquAdvantage salmon is the first GMO in the United States.

___F___ **4.** All GMO grains and vegetables grow faster than non-GMO grains and vegetables.

___T___ **5.** Some countries do not allow GMOs.

___T___ **6.** Farmers who grow GMO corn use more herbicides than they did before they had
GMO corn.

___T___ **7.** In areas where GMO corn is grown, there are fewer butterflies than there were
20 years ago.

___T___ **8.** Superweeds are very difficult to kill.

___F___ **9.** The AquAdvantage salmon company is worried about environmental problems that the
new fish might create.

MAKE INFERENCES

INFERRING FACTS

An **inference** is an educated guess about something that is not directly stated in the text.
Sometimes it is possible for readers to **infer facts** from a text even when these facts are not
directly stated.

Look at the example and read the explanation.

• "And for a hungry world population, more salmon means cheaper salmon and better health for
many people." (*paragraph 2*)

Which fact can you infer from this text?

a. AquAdvantage fish are healthier to eat than other fish.

b. Salmon is a very healthy food.
(*The correct answer is **b**.*)

If salmon is cheaper, more people will be able to buy and eat it. The text says this will result in
better health for many people. So we can **infer** that salmon is a healthy food.

Read each quote from the reading. Which fact can you infer from it? Circle the correct answer.

1. "If the U.S. government approves AquAdvantage salmon, it will be the first GMO fish in U.S. supermarkets. But Americans have been eating GMO vegetables and grains for almost 20 years." *(paragraph 3)*

   a. Most Americans don't care or don't know that they are eating GMOs.

   b. Since GMO vegetables are safe, GMO fish is probably safe, too.

2. "The butterfly population is 80% lower in these areas than it was 20 years ago. Herbicides kill a wild plant called milkweed, and butterflies need milkweed to live. So the GMO corn is changing the whole food chain in these areas." *(paragraph 7)*

   a. GMO corn kills butterflies.

   b. GMO corn changes the environment in a negative way in the areas where it grows.

3. "The AquAdvantage company tells us that the new fish will not create any problems for the environment. But can we believe them? Monsanto, the company that created GMO corn, did not predict any problems from GMO corn 20 years ago either." *(paragraph 8)*

   a. The AquAdvantage company does not know if the new fish will create problems.

   b. AquAdvantage is a more honest company than Monsanto.

Now discuss your answers with a partner.

EXPRESS OPINIONS

Discuss the questions with a partner. Give your opinions. Then share your answers with the class.

1. If you see AquAdvantage salmon in the market, will you buy it? Why or why not?

2. Do you think that GMOs are a good idea? Why or why not?

3. If countries say no to GMOs, what are some of the other ways to help farmers create more food with the same amount of land and work?

▪▪▪▪▪▪▪▪▪▪▪▪▪▪▪▪▪▪▪▪▪▪▪▪▪▪▪▪ *GO TO* MyEnglishLab *TO GIVE YOUR OPINION ABOUT ANOTHER QUESTION.*

READD

1 Look at the boldfaced words in the reading and think about the questions.

1. Which words do you know the meaning of?

2. Can you use any of the words in a sentence?

2 TravelingTipsForYou is a website that posts tips for travelers to various countries. Read this page to help travelers to the United States understand all the food choices in that country.

TRAVELING TIPS FOR YOU
Making Sense of the American Diet

1 Hamburgers and french fries are known all over the world as "typical American food." But when you travel in the United States, you will see that Americans choose many different kinds of **diets**. As a matter of fact, many Americans spend a lot of time thinking very hard about how and what they eat. They think that the traditional American diet is bad for their health and bad for the environment. As a result, you will see many labels and descriptions of food that might seem confusing. Here is a short guide to help you understand some of the choices:

2 **ORGANIC** foods are grown with no pesticides[1] or herbicides. There are also no GMOs in organic food. People who choose organic foods think they are better for their health and for the environment.

3 **VEGETARIAN** food contains no meat. People choose a vegetarian diet for a number of reasons. Some believe that eating meat is not good for their health. Others have environmental reasons. They believe eating plants is better for the environment. Cows and other "meat" animals at the top of the food chain need lots of food, water, and energy. Carrots, beans, and potatoes, on the lower end of the food chain, need much less. Still others believe that people should not eat animals for **ethical** reasons. They believe that humans should not kill animals for any reason.

---

[1] **pesticides:** chemicals that kill insects

(continued on next page)

4   **VEGAN** foods contain nothing at all from animals: no meat, no milk, no eggs, no honey, and no butter, for example. Reasons for eating a vegan diet are very similar to reasons for eating a vegetarian diet. But vegan eaters don't think that humans should use animals for food at all.

5   **LOCAL** food is grown less than 100 miles from you. Local food is usually very fresh. And buying it helps nearby farms and other businesses. People who eat local food also care about the environment. They don't want to eat food that must travel far by trucks, boats, and planes because it uses too much gasoline. This causes more pollution.

6   **LOW-FAT** foods have very little fat (for example, butter or oil) in them. People who are trying to lose weight, or people who have heart disease[2] often eat low-fat diets. Many Americans have heart disease or are overweight, so low-fat diets and foods are very common in the U.S.

7   **GLUTEN-FREE** foods contain no gluten. Gluten[3] is in wheat and many other grains. People with a gluten-free diet are usually **allergic** to gluten. They might get very bad stomachaches if they eat it.

_____

[2] **heart disease:** sickness of the heart that can lead to heart attacks or other heart problems
[3] **gluten:** a protein in grains, especially wheat, that helps make bread rise

COMPREHENSION

Match the description of a person on the left with a type of diet on the right.

1. Someone who doesn't want to eat animals, but who likes

   milk, eats _____.

2. Someone who doesn't want to eat animals or anything made

   by animals eats _____.

3. Someone who wants to lose weight eats _____.

4. Someone who doesn't want to eat GMOs and pesticides eats

   _____.

5. Someone who wants to support farmers in nearby areas eats

   _____.

6. Someone who is allergic to wheat eats _____.

a. organic food

b. vegetarian food

c. vegan food

d. local food

e. low-fat food

f. gluten-free food

GO TO MyEnglishLab _FOR MORE VOCABULARY PRACTICE_

READING SKILL

1 Look at paragraph 4 of Reading Two again. What are the foods that are not allowed in a vegan diet? Underline the words.

SCANNING FOR INFORMATION

Sometimes a reader may look for a specific piece of information within the text. This is called **scanning**. To scan a text is to quickly move your eyes over the words until you find the information you are looking for.

For example:

If you want to find the foods that are not allowed in the vegan diet, you are not going to read every word of the paragraph about vegan foods. Instead, you will quickly move your eyes over the words until you find the names of foods that are not allowed.

- "**VEGAN** foods contain nothing at all from animals: no meat, no milk, no eggs, no honey, and no butter, for example. Reasons for eating a vegan diet are very similar to reasons for eating a vegetarian diet. But vegan eaters don't think that humans should use animals for food at all." *(paragraph 4)*

Scanning this paragraph allowed you to quickly find the information you were looking for "no meat, no milk, no eggs, no honey, and no butter."

2 Work with a partner to answer the questions below about Reading Two.

1. Scan paragraph 2 for this information: What two items make food non-organic?

2. Scan paragraph 5 for this information: To be local, food must be grown within how many miles?

3. Scan paragraph 6 for this information: Who are the people who eat low-fat foods?

■■■■■■■■■■■■■■■■■■■■■■■■■■■■■■■■■■■■■■■ *GO TO* MyEnglishLab *FOR MORE SKILL PRACTICE.*

CONNECT THE READINGS

STEP 1: Organize

Read the list of statements based on Readings One (**R1**) and Two (**R2**). Then complete the chart with the appropriate statements to give reasons for eating each type of food.

a. Food grown without pesticides and herbicides does not harm the food chain.

b. Food grown without pesticides and herbicides is better for your body.

c. It's fresher and tastes better.

d. It uses less gasoline.

(continued on next page)

e. Americans have a lot of heart disease and are often overweight.

f. People who have allergies get sick if they eat gluten.

g. Farmers can grow more on less land.

h. People should not kill animals.

~~**i.** Many people in the world are hungry and do not have enough food.~~

j. Meat is not good for our health.

k. It helps local businesses and farms.

l. Food that is lower on the food chain uses less water, land, and energy.

TYPE OF FOOD	REASON IT IS GOOD FOR THE ENVIRONMENT	REASON IT IS GOOD FOR HEALTH	OTHER REASONS IT IS GOOD TO GROW OR EAT
1. GMO	X	_i_	_____
2. ORGANIC	_____	_____	X
3. VEGETARIAN / VEGAN	_____	_____	_____
4. LOW-FAT	X	_____	X
5. LOCAL	_____	X	_____ , _____
6. GLUTEN-FREE	X	_____	X

STEP 2: Synthesize

Complete the conversation in an online chat room. Use ideas from the two readings and the chart in Step 1. Then give your opinion.

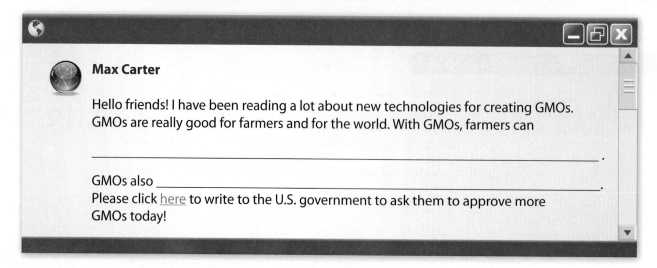

Max Carter

Hello friends! I have been reading a lot about new technologies for creating GMOs. GMOs are really good for farmers and for the world. With GMOs, farmers can

_____ .

GMOs also _____
Please click here to write to the U.S. government to ask them to approve more GMOs today!

Kaia Simms

I completely disagree, Max! I think everybody should eat an organic diet. Organic food

doesn't have _____. GMOs are bad for the

environment. They _____

_____

_____.

Jacob Lee

Yes. Farmers need GMO grains because they need to feed them to the animals they

raise for meat. But I think eating meat is unnecessary. A vegan diet is better for the

environment and for your health!

For example, _____

_____

_____.

_____

[*your name*]

[*your opinion*]

_____

_____

_____.

GO TO MyEnglishLab *TO CHECK WHAT YOU LEARNED.*

VOCABULARY

REVIEW

Complete each sentence with the correct word from the box.

allergic	diet	grains	resist
~~approve~~	environment	insects	weeds
benefits	ethical	population	
complex	food chain		

1. In our restaurant, the chef controls everything. She needs to _____*approve*_____ every plate that goes to the customers. If she sees just one piece of lettuce out of place, the plate goes back.

2. I've lost weight, I spend less money on food, and I have more energy. There are lots of _____ to going on a vegetarian diet.

3. If Betsy eats peanuts, she has trouble breathing and needs to go to the hospital immediately. She is _____ to peanuts.

4. Jenny is a vegetarian. Her reasons are _____. She actually thinks it is OK to eat animals, but she thinks that most farms in the United States give animals too many chemicals and medicines.

5. Something is eating the tomatoes in my garden! I am not sure if it is birds or _____.

6. If you eat well and exercise, your body will _____ a lot of sicknesses.

7. When the ship sank, gasoline and oil filled the lake. We couldn't swim there for a long time because the _____ was destroyed.

8. I can't keep the _____ away. They are growing faster than my vegetables. I guess I'll have to start using some herbicides to help.

9. Lions, bears, and humans all eat other animals. But nothing eats them. They are at the top of the _____.

10. In many cities, small birds are disappearing. Some say it's because the cat

_____ is getting bigger.

11. I believe people need to be kind to animals while they are alive, even if we eat them

later. It is our _____ responsibility.

12. I love this bread. It's made from seven different _____.

13. Today I ate a little ice cream, but that was very unusual. In general, I eat a low-fat

_____.

EXPAND

1 Complete the chart with the correct word forms. Use a dictionary if necessary. An **X** indicates that there is no form in that category.

	NOUN	VERB	ADJECTIVE	ADVERB
1.	allergy	X	*allergic*	X
2.		approve	approving	approvingly
3.	environment	X		environmentally
4.	ethics	X		
5.		resist		X

2 Complete the sentences using the correct form of the words. Choose from the forms in parentheses.

1. Tobias is a man with strong _____.
   (ethics / ethical)

2. Neven is _____ to honey.
   (allergy / allergic)

3. When Amy finished playing her piano concert, her mother smiled

_____.
   (approve / approvingly)

4. Some people think that if you eat oranges you will _____ colds
   (resistant / resist)

and flu.

5. The National Park Service is an _____ organization.
   (environment / environmental)

6. Some insects have _____ to pesticides.
   (resistance / resist)

7. Most children ask their parents for _____ before going over to a
   (approval / approve)

friend's house.

Helen and Jeremy are asking the concierge at their hotel for ideas about where to go for dinner. Complete the conversation. Use words from the box.

approved	complex	environment	grains	population
benefit	diet	ethical	organic	resist

Where Shall We Go to Dinner?

HELEN: Hello! We are looking for a place to eat dinner. There will be four of us. Can you recommend a good restaurant?

CONCIERGE: Earl's Barbecue is the best place in town, and it is just one block away.

JEREMY: Barbecue? That sounds great!

HELEN: We can't go to a meat restaurant because Shayla _____

_____ .

CONCIERGE: Oh well, in that case try Italian Colors. They have lots of pasta and several vegetarian dishes.

JEREMY: A pasta restaurant is not good for my mom because _____

_____ .

HELEN: And I prefer _____

_____ .

CONCIERGE: Wow! _____

_____ .

JEREMY: _____ .

GO TO MyEnglishLab FOR MORE VOCABULARY PRACTICE.

GRAMMAR

1 Read the online restaurant review of an all organic / vegetarian / local food restaurant in Brooklyn, New York. Underline the sentences with **too**.

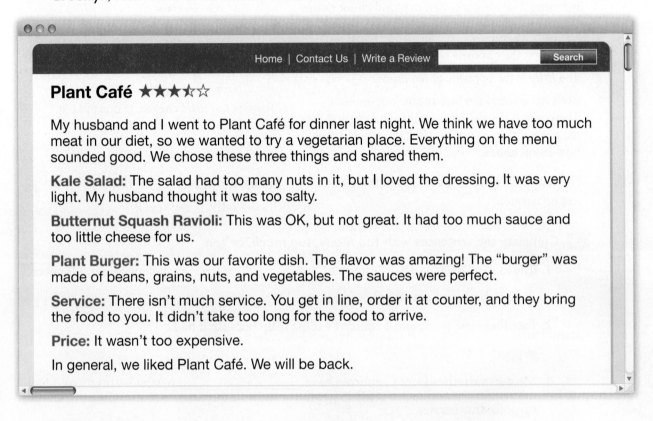

Home | Contact Us | Write a Review   [   ] Search

Plant Café ★★★½☆

My husband and I went to Plant Café for dinner last night. We think we have too much meat in our diet, so we wanted to try a vegetarian place. Everything on the menu sounded good. We chose these three things and shared them.

Kale Salad: The salad had too many nuts in it, but I loved the dressing. It was very light. My husband thought it was too salty.

Butternut Squash Ravioli: This was OK, but not great. It had too much sauce and too little cheese for us.

Plant Burger: This was our favorite dish. The flavor was amazing! The "burger" was made of beans, grains, nuts, and vegetables. The sauces were perfect.

Service: There isn't much service. You get in line, order it at counter, and they bring the food to you. It didn't take too long for the food to arrive.

Price: It wasn't too expensive.

In general, we liked Plant Café. We will be back.

2 Read again the sentences that you underlined in the review. Then read each statement. Decide if it is true or false. Write **T** (true) or **F** (false) next to it.

_____ 1. The writer usually eats meat.

_____ 2. The writer's husband didn't like the taste of the salad dressing.

_____ 3. The writer loved the ravioli.

_____ 4. The writer had to wait a long time for her food.

_____ 5. The food costs a lot at this restaurant.

TOO MUCH / TOO MANY / TOO + ADJECTIVE

Too many and *too much* mean "more than the right amount." These words usually have a negative meaning. Use *too many* before plural count nouns. Use *too much* before non-count nouns.

plural count noun
There are *too many* nuts. (I don't like it.)
non-count noun
There is *too much* sauce. (I don't like it.)

Too few is the opposite of *too many*.

Too little is the opposite of *too much*.

Both *too few* and *too little* mean "not enough." These words usually have a negative meaning. Use *too few* with count nouns. Use *too little* with non-count nouns.

plural count noun
There are *too few* waiters. (Service is slow.)
non-count noun
There is *too little* cheese. (I don't like it.)

Use *too* + **adjective** to say that something has a negative result.

It's *too* expensive. (I can't buy it.)
It's *too* salty. (I can't eat it.)

3 Complete the sentences with **too many**, **too much**, or **too**.

1. The food at Neetcha Thai Restaurant had _____too many_____ peanuts on it. I'll never go back because I am allergic to peanuts.

2. I ate there last week, and I couldn't eat the soup because it had _____ pepper.

3. Most strawberries from California have _____ pesticides on them. I buy organic strawberries.

4. Eating healthy is _____ difficult for me. I just eat food that is cheap and easy!

5. The pasta was _____ salty. I almost couldn't eat it.

6. You put _____ milk in the coffee. I only wanted a little bit.

7. Jennifer eats _____ sugar. That's why her teeth are bad.

8. I think that my boss drinks _____ coffee. He is always very nervous.

9. The food at Flavors of India is _____ spicy for me. I can't eat it.

10. The dinner was delicious, but I can't finish everything on my plate. I took _____ food.

4 Finish the sentences using **too many**, **too much** or **too** and the words in parentheses. Add a sentence to each item about the negative result.

1. Pier 23 Café had (people) _too many people. There was no table for us, so we left._

2. The prices at La Ferme Restaurant are (high) _____ .

   _____ .

3. Most Americans eat (junk food) _____ .

   _____ .

   _____ .

4. I ate (cookies) _____ .

   _____ .

5. Vegan people think that most of us eat (meat) _____ .

   _____ .

■■■■■■■■■■■■ *GO TO* MyEnglishLab *FOR MORE GRAMMAR PRACTICE AND TO CHECK WHAT YOU LEARNED.*

FINAL WRITING TASK

In this unit, you read about new ways of growing foods and new types of diet.

Now you are going to **write a paragraph about your diet.** Describe your diet with a general statement. Then give some examples of the types of food you eat and tell why you choose this diet. Explain the health, environmental, ethical, or other reasons. Explain any problems with this diet. Use the vocabulary and grammar from the unit.*

---

* For Alternative Writing Topics, see page 131. These topics can be used in place of the writing topic for this unit or as homework. The alternative topics relate to the theme of the unit but may not target the same grammar or rhetorical structures taught in the unit.

PREPARE TO WRITE: Using an e-Chart

An **e-chart** can help you organize your writing. Write the topic on the single line on the left and use the three lines for the details.

1 Look at the model e-chart.

	Detail 1: examples of the foods in this diet
Topic: the type of diet you have	**Detail 2:** the reason the author chooses this diet
	Detail 3: problems with this diet

	cereal, candy bars, packaged food, restaurant food
No-cooking diet	I am a bad cook, and I don't have time.
	Restaurant food and packaged food are not healthy.

2 Create an e-chart for your diet.

WRITE: Giving Reasons

When you explain your choices, you **give reasons**. You must answer the question: *Why?*

1 Read each paragraph. Then answer the questions.

I have a "no-cooking" diet. This means I only eat food that I don't have to cook. At home, I eat a lot of cereal and snacks like crackers and chips. Sometimes I eat fruit, too. I eat at restaurants often. There is no good reason for my diet. It's mostly because I am a terrible cook, and I have very little time to cook because I am going to school and working. My diet is not very healthy. It is very high-fat, high-salt, and high-sugar. I am going to try to learn to cook some simple dishes this summer when my sister comes to visit. Then maybe I can have a "simple cooking" diet. It will be healthier!

1. What kind of diet does this author have? _____

2. Underline the sentences that explain *why* she chooses this diet. What words or phrases in these sentences tell you that the author is giving her reasons? _____

_____

I have a mostly Chinese diet. It includes lots of vegetables, some spices and sauces, a little meat, lots of rice, and green tea. I follow this diet mostly because I am used to it. My mom is Chinese, and she is a good cook, so I learned to cook from her. I also think that a Chinese diet is healthy and good for the environment because it has lots of vegetables and not too much meat. It has lots of vitamins, and it is low on the food chain. But I also like ice cream, and that is not part of the Chinese diet. My mom always tells me ice cream is very bad for me, but I eat it about once a week because it is just so delicious!

1. What kind of diet does this author have? _____

2. Underline the sentences that explain *why* she is on this diet. What words or phrases in these sentences tell you that the author is giving her reasons? _____

_____

2 Now use your e-chart to write the first draft of your paragraph.

REVISE: Expressing Contrasting Ideas

In a paragraph that explains the reasons for a choice, the author also often gives the reader information about a **contrasting idea**. Use words such as *but* or *however* to let the reader know you are introducing a contrasting idea.

1 Read the paragraph. Then answer the questions.

I eat only vegetarian food. This means I eat no chicken, fish, beef, or pork. I think it's better for my health to eat only fruits and vegetables. I also have ethical reasons. I think it's bad to kill other animals so that I can live. I want to eat vegetarian all the time for the reasons above, but sometimes it's too difficult. Traveling to other countries or eating at my friend's house are two times when it's very hard to be vegetarian. How can I say no to a meal someone has made for me?

1. What kind of diet does this author have?

2. Double underline the sentences that show the difficulties in staying on this diet.

3. What word tells you that the author is changing from giving reasons to explaining the problems?

2 Read the paragraph and decide where the contrasting word **however** belongs. Insert a comma after **however** if it starts a sentence.

I am trying to eat a low-junk food diet. _____ I eat carrots or apples when I want a snack. _____ For lunch, I have just a simple salad. _____ I'm doing this because I have very bad eating habits, and I know that junk food is bad for my health. _____ I know that all of those foods are very high-sugar, high-salt, and high-fat. _____ I ate no junk food for one whole week last month. _____ I felt much healthier, and I lost three pounds! _____ I still love the taste of things like potato chips, pizza, chocolate, and french fries. I think about them all the time! It is really difficult not to eat those things.

3 Now go back to the first draft of your paragraph and use contrasting words to introduce the problems with your diet. Make sure you use the correct punctuation.

■■■■■■■■■■■■■■■■■■■■■■■■■■■■■■■■■■■■ GO TO MyEnglishLab FOR MORE SKILL PRACTICE.

EDIT: Writing the Final Draft

Go to MyEnglishLab and write the final draft of your paragraph. Carefully edit it for grammatical and mechanical errors such as spelling, capitalization, and punctuation. Make sure you use some of the vocabulary and grammar from the unit. Use the checklist to help you write your final draft. Then submit your paragraph to your teacher.

FINAL DRAFT CHECKLIST

❑ Does your paragraph describe the kind of diet you eat?

❑ Does it explain why you choose to eat that way and some of the difficulties with the diet?

❑ Do you give good reasons for choosing this diet?

❑ Do you use contrasting words to introduce the problems with this diet?

❑ Do you use correct punctuation?

❑ Do the supporting sentences give explanations?

❑ Do you use *too much / too many* or *too* + adjective correctly?

❑ Do you use new vocabulary that you learned in this unit?

UNIT PROJECT

You are going to *create a shopping guide for your town* to help shoppers find the food they want. Research some local shops to find out what kinds of food they sell. Follow these steps:

STEP 1: As a class, develop a survey of items you are interested in buying at grocery stores. The survey will look like a checklist:

Name of store: _____

Address: _____

Supermarket checklist:

_____ Organic meats

_____ Local meats

_____ Fruits and vegetables

_____ Organic fruits and vegetables

_____ Local fruits and vegetables

_____ Bread

_____ Gluten-free bread

_____ (*your ideas*)

_____ (*your ideas*)

STEP 2: With a partner, choose a local supermarket or food store. Make sure that each pair in the class chooses a different store.

STEP 3: Visit the store's website or the actual store. Check off the items that the store carries. (You might also write down some prices.)

STEP 4: Compare your findings with what your classmates found. Create a shopper's guide with all the information from your research in one place. You might create a page for each store, or a large chart listing each store and type of food, for example:

	ORGANIC MEATS	LOCAL MEATS	FRESH FRUITS AND VEGETABLES	ORGANIC FRUITS AND VEGETABLES	LOCAL FRUITS AND VEGETABLES	BREAD	GLUTEN-FREE BREAD
SHOP #1							
SHOP #2							
SHOP #3							
SHOP #4							
SHOP #5							

ALTERNATIVE WRITING TOPICS

Write about one of the topics. Use the vocabulary and grammar from the unit.

1. Is it possible to be a locavore (a person who eats only local food—within 100 miles) in your town? Write a paragraph describing what a locavore can eat in your town and if you think it's a good idea for people to eat this way.

2. Is GMO food legal in your country? Is it legal to sell it without "GMO" labels? Research online the relationship your country has to GMO foods today and in the past 20 years. Write a short paragraph describing what you learned.

3. For some people on special diets, traveling can be difficult. But for most people, discovering new foods is one of the pleasures of travel. In one paragraph, describe a new food experience you had while visiting a new place. Where were you? What was the food, and how was it prepared? How did you choose this food? What was special about it? Would you recommend this food to others?

■■■■■■■■■■■■■■■■■■ GO TO MyEnglishLab TO WRITE ABOUT ONE OF THE ALTERNATIVE TOPICS, WATCH A VIDEO ABOUT A FOOD COMPANY, AND TAKE THE UNIT 5 ACHIEVEMENT TEST. ■■■■■■■■■■■■■■

THE
HEART OF A
Hero

1 FOCUS ON THE TOPIC

1. Hercules is a Greek hero. In the many stories describing his adventures and combats, Hercules is always extraordinarily strong and courageous. What quality do you think makes someone a hero?

2. Describe a hero from a story from your culture.

3. Do you have a favorite hero from a folk tale,[1] book, or movie? Who? Why is this person or character a hero?

---

[1] **folk tale**: a short story that comes from the spoken word or oral tradition

■■■■■■■■■■■■■■■■■■■■■■■■■■■■■■■■ *GO TO* MyEnglishLab *TO CHECK WHAT YOU KNOW.*

VOCABULARY

1 Read short descriptions of some famous heroes. Try to understand the boldfaced words without looking them up in a dictionary.

1. **Odysseus** is a hero from Greek stories famous for his **journey** home to his family from the Trojan War.

2. **Mulan** is a hero from Chinese stories. She is famous for taking her father's job as a soldier. She did not have strength, but she was a good soldier because of her **intelligence**. She used her brains to help the army win.

3. **James Bond** is a hero from British stories who fights bad guys. In every James Bond movie, there is always a moment where we see him **struggling** hard to beat the bad guys. He is a good fighter and always wins.

4. **Iron Man** is a superhero known for the power from his metal suit. In each adventure he helps people get out of **dangerous** situations.

5. **Bilbo Baggins**, the hero of the story *The Hobbit*, **succeeds** in returning the stolen gold to his friend, Thorin.

6. **Goku** is a Japanese Manga hero. He is known for his strength. He uses his strength to bring people to **safety** and create peace.

7. **King Arthur** is one of Britain's most famous heroes. He had a **mentor**, Merlin. Merlin was a wise man who taught King Arthur how to be a king and how to be a man.

8. **Percy Jackson** is a hero from an American book. The death of his mother **affects** him deeply. He is changed forever as a result.

9. **Jim Hawkins** is the young hero of the story *Treasure Island*. Jim helps the good guys find the gold hidden on an island and return it to its owners.

10. **Robin Hood** is a British hero who helps the poor at every **opportunity**. Whenever he can, he steals money from the rich and gives it to the poor.

2 Match the words on the left with the definitions on the right.

_e_ **1.** journey   **a.** to do well; to do what you tried to do

_____ **2.** intelligence   **b.** to touch or to make someone feel strong emotions

_____ **3.** struggle   **c.** a group of valuable things such as gold, silver, and jewelry

_____ **4.** dangerous   **d.** the state of being free from danger or harm

_____ **5.** succeed   ~~**e.** a trip, usually a long one~~

_____ **6.** safety   **f.** likely to harm people

_____ **7.** mentor   **g.** a chance or a time to do something

_____ **8.** affect   **h.** the ability to learn and understand things

_____ **9.** treasure   **i.** to try to do something that is difficult or to fight something

_____ **10.** opportunity   **j.** an older and wiser person who helps a younger person

GO TO MyEnglishLab FOR MORE VOCABULARY PRACTICE.

PREVIEW

You are going to read a college student's essay on the work of Joseph Campbell, a professor of literature and religion. Campbell is famous for his ideas about hero stories from around the world. Before you read, look at the list below. Check (✓) three things you think Campbell might say about heroes.

Heroes . . .

❑ are good.

❑ are handsome / beautiful.

❑ have special abilities.

❑ are strong.

❑ help others.

❑ are scared.

❑ go out into the world.

❑ fight bad people.

❑ do something difficult.

Now read the essay.

Natalie Carson
English 1A

WHAT IS A HERO?

1   Joseph Campbell (1904–1987) spent his life answering this question. Campbell was a professor of literature and religion at Sarah Lawrence College in New York. He studied and taught hero stories from around the world. Over the years, he noticed that a lot of myths—a kind of hero story—are very similar. In old myths or new ones, whether from Asia, Africa, or South America, the world's hero stories all have the same basic shape. The details of the stories may change, but every hero story has the same three parts.

2   During the first part of any hero story, the hero starts a **journey**. This can be a trip from one country to another. It can be an adventure into outer space. It can be a journey into a dream world. Often the hero does not, at first, want to go on this journey. But in the end, he agrees. He leaves the **safety** of his home, friends, and family and goes to this new place. This place is very different from the hero's home and is often dark and **dangerous**. Sometimes there is a **mentor** or a teacher who helps the hero understand this new place. The mentor gives the hero the tools or information he needs. For example, a kind old lady on the road may give our hero a map for his journey. A stranger may give the young hero the key to the door of the enemy king's castle.[1]

3   The second part in the hero story is the most exciting. This is when the hero must pass some kind of test or challenge. A common example of a test is fighting a monster. In these stories, the monster is much bigger and stronger than our hero. The hero and the readers do not, at first, believe he can kill the monster. Other common challenges include solving a problem or facing a fear such as the fear of snakes. In any challenge, the hero must use his strength, his **intelligence**, or his heart to pass the test. He must kill the dragon, answer the question, or trust his feelings. Of course, in the end, he always **succeeds**.

4   Finally, in the third part of the hero story, the hero returns home. He is a different person now and brings what he has acquired or learned on his journey—wealth, knowledge, and wisdom—to share with his family and friends. When he returns home, others are also **affected** by his journey. Sometimes his enemies are embarrassed. Sometimes his family and his friends become rich. Sometimes the hero's town becomes free.

5   Campbell believes that the adventure of the hero is the adventure of being alive. Campbell spent his life studying myths because he loved the stories and believed they were important. He believed that the hero's journey is similar to a person's life. All people live through difficult **struggles** (the test or challenge) and must use their strength, intelligence, and heart to succeed. He says that by going down into the darkness, we find the **treasures** of life. He explains that the cave[2] we are afraid to enter has the treasure we are looking for and that when we stumble,[3] then we will find gold. In short, Campbell believes that **opportunities** to find deeper powers within ourselves come when life seems most difficult.

---

1 **castle:** a very large stone building built in past times to protect the king from attack
2 **cave:** a large dark hole in the side of a cliff or under the ground
3 **stumble:** to hit something with your foot while you are walking so that you almost fall

MAIN IDEAS

1 Look again at the Preview on page 135. How did your predictions help you understand the story?

2 Circle the word or phrase that best completes each statement about an idea discussed in the essay.

1. Hero stories are **the same / different** all over the world.

2. Hero stories usually have **two / three** main parts.

3. Hero stories are important because they are **similar to / different from** life in general.

DETAILS

Check (✓) the words or phrases that <u>always</u> belong to the three parts of the hero story.

Part One

❑ a journey   ❑ leaving home

❑ a castle   ❑ a mentor / teacher

❑ an adventure   ❑ coming home

❑ a dream

Part Two

❑ a test / challenge   ❑ facing a fear

❑ a monster   ❑ snakes

❑ a fight   ❑ succeeding at the challenge

❑ solving a problem

Part Three

❑ returning home   ❑ wisdom

❑ bringing what he / she gained   ❑ others are changed, too

❑ wealth   ❑ enemies killed

❑ knowledge   ❑ friends become rich

MAKE INFERENCES

INFERRING MEANING FROM METAPHORS

An **inference** is an educated guess about something that is not directly stated in the text. Sometimes a writer suggests a complex idea by using a **metaphor** (word/phrase creating an image) that makes the complex idea simpler and clearer.

Look at the example and read the explanation.

- "... the cave we are afraid to enter has the treasure we are looking for ..." *(paragraph 5)*

Cave here is used as a metaphor. From the image of a cave, the reader **infers** the dark, difficult things in a person's life, such as sadness, poverty, anger, poor health, or any other negative human experience. These are complex things to describe. The author simplifies these complicated ideas by using the word *cave* because this word holds all the feeling and meaning of those difficult things.

After reading the text closely, especially certain words or phrases that are used as metaphors, we can **infer** the full meaning of the complex ideas the author wants to convey.

Read the quotes from paragraph 5 of the reading. The underlined word in each one is used as a metaphor. What complex idea does the author want to convey here? Write the meaning of the metaphor on the line.

Metaphor	Meaning
1. "... the cave we are afraid to enter has the <u>treasure</u> we are looking for ..."	_____
2. "... when we <u>stumble</u>, then we will find gold."	_____
3. "... when we stumble, then we will find <u>gold</u>."	_____

EXPRESS OPINIONS

Discuss the questions below in a small group. Give your opinions. Then share your answers with the class.

1. Do you agree with Campbell's quote in the last paragraph? Why?

2. Think of a hero story from your culture. Does it follow the pattern that Joseph Campbell describes for all hero stories throughout the world? Explain.

■■■■■■■■■■■■■■■■■■■■■■■■ GO TO MyEnglishLab TO GIVE YOUR OPINION ABOUT ANOTHER QUESTION.

READ

1 Look at the boldfaced words and phrases in the reading and think about the questions.

1. Which words or phrases do you know the meaning of?

2. Can you use any of the words or phrases in a sentence?

2 Now read the blog by pre-med student Alice Ogrodnik.

Book Review: *Harry Potter and the Sorcerer's Stone*

HOME

CONTACT

About Me

My name is Alice Ogrodnik. I'm a 22-year-old senior in college, studying biology. After I graduate, I am going to medical school to become a medical geneticist. I'm a big reader and use reading as a way to relax from all the hard class work.

1 I just finished reading *Harry Potter and the Sorcerer's Stone* by J.K. Rowling. I know I'm a little behind most of you. Most people I know read these books years ago. In fact, I think a lot of people my age who never read books for fun, started reading BECAUSE of the Harry Potter books. But I wasn't like those people. I read books all the time. So when everyone started reading *Harry Potter*, I told myself the books were bad. I told myself I read GOOD books, not silly stuff. Well, silly me. I just finished the first one and guess what? It was great. Read on to hear why . . .

2 First of all, I love a story where the main character is just a normal kid. No, not all kids are wizards.[1] But all kids go to school, make friends, play

---

[1] **wizard**: a man who teaches and practices magic

(continued on next page)

games, and have teachers they love and teachers they hate. Only in Harry's world all this happens at an amazing place called Hogwarts School of Witchcraft and Wizardry. Here, Harry makes two best friends, Ron and Hermione. They go to cool classes like Potions (**magic** drinks) and the History of Magic. They get to play a magical sport called Quidditch, which seems really fun. Harry hates his potions teacher, Snape, and he loves the headmaster, Dumbledore. Harry has no parents. When he was a baby, they died **protecting** him from the wizard Lord Voldemort. So Dumbledore acts like a father to Harry.

3   The second reason I loved this book is because it is a great **adventure**. One day, Harry and his two friends find something strange at their school: a large three-headed dog. They learn that the dog is protecting something called the Sorcerer's Stone. This magical stone takes Hermione, Ron, and Harry on a long journey that leads them to the basement of Hogwarts. Here they must pass many tests. If they fail to pass all the tests, Lord Voldemort will get the Stone, live forever, and rule the wizard world. The challenges are really exciting! In one room they find a magical plant that tries to strangle them. In another room they must play and win a life-sized game of wizard chess.[2] In the next room, they must drink dangerous potions. Because there's only enough potion for one, Harry takes it and goes on alone. When he finally arrives in the last room, Harry meets Lord Voldemort—the most dangerous wizard of all time. Will Harry be able to win? Harry does his best in a confrontation with Voldemort. At last Voldemort reaches for Harry's arm. Harry thinks it is over. He falls to the ground and everything goes black.

4   In the last chapter, Harry wakes up in bed with his friends nearby and Dumbledore smiling down at him. Dumbledore explains that Harry didn't **fail**. When his mother saved him from Voldemort with her life, she gave Harry the most powerful magic in the world. With it, he **defeated** Voldemort. At least for now.

5   This brings me to the third reason I loved this book: Harry is all set to have another adventure because he must meet Voldemort again. . . . I can't wait to read *Harry Potter and the Chamber of Secrets*!

---

[2] **chess:** a board game requiring deep thinking

COMPREHENSION

Put the following statements in the order they happen in the story of *Harry Potter and Sorcerer's Stone*.

a.   __1__   Harry's parents die.

b.   _____   Lord Voldemort is defeated.

c.   _____   Harry makes friends with Ron and Hermione.

d. _____ Harry wakes up next to his friends and Dumbledore.

e. _____ Harry and his friends find the three-headed dog.

f. _____ Harry and his friends win at wizard chess.

g. _____ Harry goes to Hogwarts.

h. _____ Harry fights Lord Voldemort.

■■■■■■■■■■■■■■■■■■■■■■■■■■■■■■■■ *GO TO* MyEnglishLab *FOR MORE VOCABULARY PRACTICE.*

READING SKILL

1 Go back to Reading Two and read the first two sentences of paragraph 3 again. What tenses are being used here? Underline the present tense once and all other tenses twice.

UNDERSTANDING THE PRESENT TENSE IN A STORY ABOUT THE PAST

As we read, we notice that **tenses** can affect how we feel about the text:

If a story is written in the **past tense**, we feel more distant from those events. Those events happened before now, so they don't matter as much.

If a story is written in the **present or present progressive tense**, we feel more connected to the events. Those events feel more immediate and so they feel more exciting and interesting.

Look at the example and read the explanation.

• "The second reason I loved this book is because it is a great adventure. One day, Harry and his two friends find something strange at their school: a large three-headed dog."
   (paragraph 3)

The first sentence is part of the blog. The main verb is *loved*. This is **past tense** because the author read this book sometime in the recent past. She loved it when she read it.

The second sentence is the start of the Harry Potter story. The verb here is *find*. This is **present tense** because the author wants to help readers feel more connected to the story.

2 Work with a partner. Read two versions of the same text from paragraph 3 of Reading Two. Underline the verbs in each version. What verb tenses are used? Why?

1. One day, Harry and his two friends find something strange at their school: a large three-headed dog. They learn that the dog is protecting something called the Sorcerer's Stone. This magical stone takes Hermione, Ron, and Harry on a long journey that leads them to the basement of Hogwarts.

2. One day, Harry and his two friends found something strange at their school: a large three-headed dog. They learned that the dog was protecting something called the Sorcerer's Stone. This magical stone took Hermione, Ron, and Harry on a long journey that led them to the basement of Hogwarts.

3 Agree or disagree with the statements about the two versions of the text.

		Agree	Disagree
1.	The paragraph in present tense is more exciting.	❏	❏
2.	The paragraph in present tense makes me feel like I'm there in the action.	❏	❏
3.	The paragraph in past tense feels like this story happened a long time ago.	❏	❏
4.	The paragraph in past tense feels more natural.	❏	❏

GO TO MyEnglishLab FOR MORE SKILL PRACTICE.

CONNECT THE READINGS

STEP 1: Organize

Reading One (**R1**) contains lots of information about all hero stories. Reading Two (**R2**) describes details of one specific hero story. Read the lists of phrases from **R1** and **R2** and place them in the correct box in the chart on the next page.

R1

~~The hero leaves on his journey.~~

The hero's family / friends are affected by what happened on the journey.

The hero returns home.

The hero doesn't believe he can succeed.

The mentor shows the hero some useful things.

The hero succeeds in his challenges by his intelligence, strength, or wisdom.

R2

~~Harry goes into the basement of Hogwarts.~~

Harry gets past the eating plant.

The world is saved from Lord Voldemort getting the Sorcerer's Stone.

Harry defeats Lord Voldemort.

Harry wins a magic game of chess.

Harry wakes up in bed with Dumbledore smiling down on him.

	FEATURES OF EVERY HERO'S STORY (R1)	FEATURES OF HARRY POTTER'S STORY (R2)
PART ONE	*The hero leaves on his journey.*	*Harry goes into the basement of Hogwarts.*
PART TWO		
PART THREE		

Mugglenet is the most popular Harry Potter website (a *muggle* is the word in the stories for a non-magical person). Complete the website discussion from the chat.

Mugglenet Chat

HPBoy: I'm taking this great literature class on Joseph Campbell. Campbell describes the classic hero stories as all having the same form. Most of the stories he talks about are really, really old. But yesterday my teacher started talking about Harry Potter! I couldn't believe it. She says Harry Potter has the same basic form of all these really old hero stories.

RedMagic: That makes sense. I heard that J.K. Rowling studied Classics[1] at university. She probably knew a lot about these old stories and used some of the ideas.

HPBoy: Yeah, she definitely had the three main parts.

RedMagic: What are those parts?

HPBoy: Well, the first part is _____

RedMagic: And the second part?

HPBoy: _____

RedMagic: And what's the second part in Harry Potter?

HPboy: _____

RedMagic: You said three parts. What's the third one, and how does it show up in Harry Potter?

HPboy: _____

_____

RedMagic: That is so cool. It makes me feel like our love for these stories is important now . . . not something childish. It makes me want to go back to reread the book to see what you're talking about. Do you think it's true for all the Harry Potter books?

_____

[1] **Classics:** the languages, literature, and history of ancient Greece and Rome

VOCABULARY

REVIEW

Complete the tale of Perseus with the words from the box.

adventure	defeats	journey	opportunity	struggle
affect	fail	magic	protect	succeeds
~~dangerous~~	intelligent	mentors	safety	treasure

Perseus is a Greek hero who lives on an island with his family. On a nearby island lives

Medusa. Medusa is a woman with hair made of snakes. She is very _____dangerous_____. When
                                                                                    1.

anyone looks upon her ugly head, they turn to stone. Many young men try to kill her. But they all

_____ because they do not turn their eyes away. They all lose their lives. One day,
      2.

(continued on next page)

the king of the land asks Perseus to go on a _____ to bring back the head of
3.

Medusa. Perseus does not want to leave the _____ of his home and family.
4.

But he decides to say yes. For Perseus, this is a(n) _____ to show his power as a
5.

young man.

On the road to find Medusa, Perseus meets two _____ who will help him.
6.

First, he meets the god Hermes. Hermes gives him _____ shoes with wings. With
7.

these shoes, Perseus can fly. Second, he meets Athena, the goddess of war. She gives him a shield[1]

to _____ himself. How can Perseus kill Medusa without looking at her? Perseus
8.

is a(n) _____ young man. He uses the shoes to fight Medusa from the air. He uses
9.

the shield as a mirror to see, so he can cut off Medusa's head without looking at her. They start to

fight. Medusa _____. She cannot win. In the end, Perseus _____
10.   11.

Medusa and _____.
12.

On the trip home, Perseus meets and falls in love with Andromeda, his true love. Together

they return to the king with Medusa's head in a bag. Perseus' _____ is
13.

over—the monster is dead and he has his _____, Andromeda. His success
14.

_____ his whole community as he becomes king.
15.

_____
[1] **shield:** a large piece of metal, wood, or other material used to protect a soldier from attack

1 Complete the chart with the correct word forms. Some categories have more than one form. Use a dictionary if necessary. An **X** indicates that there is no form in the category.

	NOUN	VERB	ADJECTIVE	ADVERB
1.	defeat		a. *defeated* b. *defeating*	X
2.		endanger	dangerous	dangerously
3.	failure		a. failed b. failing	failingly
4.	magic	X	a. magical b. magic	magically
5.	a. protection b. protector	protect		X
6.	safety		safe	
7.		succeed	successful	

2 Complete the sentences using the correct form of the word in parentheses.

1. Thor, a superhero, has a _____ hammer.
    (magic)

2. Katniss Everdeen is very _____ of her younger sister, Primrose.
    (protect)

3. Perseus comes _____ close to looking at the face of Medusa and
    (danger)
    turning to stone.

4. Harry Potter _____ completes the challenges in the basement
    (success)
    of Hogwarts.

5. Robin Hood _____ rescues Lady Marion from the King's men.
    (safety)

6. The Iron Giant _____ to hide himself in the junk yard.
    (failure)

7. Lord Voldemort tries to _____ Harry Potter and for a second
    (defeat)
    time _____.
    (failure)

CREATE

makeyourownhero.com is a website for story writers. Use words from the box to complete the blog post and comments on a recent story that a writer posted on the site.

adventure	fail	mentor	struggle
affect	intelligence	opportunity	succeed
dangerous	journey	protect	treasure
defeats	magic	safety	

🌐   ⬜ ⬜ ❎

makeyourownhero FORUM

Golemsays: I think FictionGuys's last post was weak. I didn't like it at all. What was the story? A young mother finds a magical stone in her garden and just keeps it? . . . I don't get it. How are we supposed to see her as any kind of hero? What do you think?

KrytoMan: I agree. Maybe the mother uses the stone to go on a long

_____ to a different land. Here she meets a _____

monster that tries to kill her and her child.

Mythmaker: Nice one. The mother and the monster can _____ to

get the child. The mother starts to _____. We think she will lose.

Then, suddenly, she finds her power and _____ the monster by

killing him with his own sword.

Norsefan: I like that idea. What about this one: _____

_____

_____

Supermannut: What if _____

_____

_____

GRAMMAR

1 Read the paragraph about Atalanta. Circle the word *when* every time you see it. Underline the verbs in each *when-* sentence.

Atalanta is a popular Greek hero. She is a great runner. She can run faster than any man or woman. Her father wants her to marry. But she doesn't want to belong to any man. When she refuses to marry, her father gets angry. They argue. Finally, she agrees to a deal. She will marry the first man who can beat her in a race. Many young men try to defeat her, but they all fail. She is too fast. One young man, Hippomeses, asks a god for help. The god tells him to throw down three golden apples on the race course. When he does this, Atalanta stops running to look at the beautiful golden apples. Hippomeses wins the race, and Atalanta marries him.

TIME CLAUSES IN PRESENT TENSE

1. We can combine two sentences that tell about time by using a **time clause** and a **main clause**. *When Hippomeses meets Atalanta* is a time clause. The time clause and the main clause are both in the same tense. Here, that tense is the **simple present**.	Hippomeses meets Atalanta. He falls in love with her. Time Clause **When** Hippomeses **meets** Atalanta, Main Clause he **falls** in love with her.
2. A clause contains a subject and a verb. A time clause contains a *time word* + subject + verb. It cannot stand alone as a sentence. It needs to be attached to an independent clause. An **independent clause** can stand alone as a sentence.	[TW] [S] [V] **When** Hippomeses **meets** Atalanta, [S] [V] he **falls** in love with her. Independent Clause He **falls** in love with her.
3. When the time clause begins the sentence, put a **comma** before the main clause. There is **no** comma when the main clause begins the sentence.	**When** Hippomeses meets Atalanta, he falls in love with her. Hippomeses falls in love with Atalanta *when* he meets her. INCORRECT: Hippomeses falls in love with Atalanta, ***when*** he meets her.

2 Read each sentence. Add a comma if the sentence needs it.

1. When I choose a book to read _____ I usually choose one with exciting adventures.

2. When I read stories to my children _____ I try to decide if the hero follows Joseph Campbell's rules.

3. My son wants to be a superhero _____ when he grows up.

4. When I travel to other countries _____ I like to learn the old stories of that culture.

5. Before Harry Potter decides to fight Voldemort _____ he gets the help of his friends, Ron and Hermione.

3 Finish the sentences. Make sure you use the correct form of the verb.

1. When Harry Potter _____ , _____.

2. Robin Hood is happy when _____.

3. Before a hero goes on a journey, he usually _____.

4. After she _____ , a hero _____.

■■■■■■■■■■■■■■■■ *GO TO* MyEnglishLab *FOR MORE GRAMMAR PRACTICE AND TO CHECK WHAT YOU LEARNED.*

FINAL WRITING TASK

In this unit, you read about heroes and hero stories. Joseph Campbell says people tell hero stories because the stories are like life: "All people live through difficult struggles (the test or challenge) and must use their strength, intelligence, and heart to succeed."

Now you are going to *write a paragraph to tell the story of a hero.* You will choose a hero (from a folk tale, book, or movie) and describe a challenge he or she faced. Then you will explain how this hero used his or her strength, intelligence, or heart to overcome a challenge. You will explain the effect of overcoming that challenge on the hero or his or her people. Use the vocabulary and grammar from this unit.*

* For Alternative Writing Topics, see page 157. These topics can be used in place of the writing topic for this unit or as homework. The alternative topics relate to the theme of the unit but may not target the same grammar or rhetorical structures taught in the unit.

PREPARE TO WRITE: Listing

Choose a hero to write about. It can be a folk hero from your culture, a comic book superhero, a movie hero, or a real-life hero. Write a **list** of the main events in his or her adventures. List them in order as in the example about the Chinese hero, Mulan:

Mulan is a hero from China from around 600 A.D.

She's the daughter of an old general.

Her father taught her how to use a knife and how to ride a horse . . . not normal for a girl

Soldiers come to town to get men to fight in the war.

Mulan's father was too old to fight.

Mulan had no older brother to send in his place.

Mulan stole her father's horse and knife.

She dressed up like a man.

She joined the army.

Mulan fought for many years.

No one knew she was a girl.

She was small.

She wasn't strong.

She was smart.

She made clever plans to help the army win the war.

After the war, the emperor offered Mulan a job that would make her rich.

Mulan wanted only to return home to her family.

Her family was happy to see her.

Her father was ill, but alive.

She dressed again in the clothes of a woman.

Friends from the army came to visit.

They learned Mulan was a woman.

She brought honor to her family.

WRITE: Outlining the Story

The writing task gives you categories to help you organize your story:

- Background
- The Challenge
- How the Hero Overcame the Challenge
- The Effects

To write your outline, you must choose only the important information from your list that matches these categories.

1 Reread the list a student wrote about the Chinese hero, Mulan. Notice what information she crossed out and how she categorized the list.

BACKGROUND

Mulan is a hero from China from around 600 A.D.

She's the daughter of an old general.

Her father taught her how to use a knife and how to ride a horse . . . not normal for a girl.

Soldiers come to town to get men to fight in the war.

CHALLENGE

Mulan's father was too old to fight.

~~Mulan had no older brother to send in her place.~~

~~Mulan stole her father's horse and knife.~~

~~She dressed up like a man.~~

She joined the army.

Mulan fought for many years.

No one knew she was a girl.

She was small.

She wasn't strong.

HOW SHE OVERCAME HER CHALLENGE

She was smart.

She made clever plans to help the army win the war.

~~After the war, the emperor offered Mulan a job that would make her rich.~~

~~Mulan wanted only to return home to her family.~~

~~Her family was happy to see her.~~

Her father was ill, but alive.

~~She dressed again in the clothes of a woman.~~

~~Friends from the army came to visit.~~

~~They learned Mulan was a woman.~~

THE EFFECT

She brought honor to her family.

Now write sentences in a list about your character. Cross out any sentences that aren't important.

2 Write the sentences that you haven't crossed out from your list in the correct section of this outline.

Background

_____

_____

_____

_____

The Challenge

_____

_____

_____

_____

How the Hero Overcame the Challenge

_____

_____

_____

_____

The Effects

_____

_____

_____

_____

_____

3 An outline can help a writer organize. In short texts, each section of the outline may be a few sentences. In longer texts, each section can be a paragraph. Read the paragraph below. Identify the parts of this paragraph.

- Underline the background information on the hero.
- Circle the information on the challenge.
- Double underline the information on how the hero overcame the challenge.
- Bracket the effects.

Mulan is a girl hero from China around 600 A.D. Her father is supposed to go to the army to fight the Huns. He is old. She is young. She decides to go to the army instead of her father. Her challenge is to pass as a boy. This is difficult because she is not very strong like the other soldiers. But she is very clever. In their first battle, when she and her men face too many enemy soldiers, her idea saves them. Mulan tells her men to make a big noise. The sound makes a wall of snow fall on the enemy soldiers. Mulan and her men win the battle. This is the first of many times when Mulan makes a plan to save her men. The leader of the soldiers is very happy with Mulan for this, and her secret is never discovered. Mulan succeeds in saving her father from fighting. Also, she brings honor to her family by being a good soldier.

4 Now write the first draft of your paragraph. Include all the information in your outline.

REVISE: Adding Explanations

Explanations and **examples** help the reader understand what the author is trying to say. They give the reader specific information to help explain the ideas.

1 Read the paragraph about Mulan again. Look at the underlined sentence. How do we know that Mulan is clever? What does the author show us that proves she is clever?

Mulan is a girl hero from China around 600 A.D. Her father is supposed to go to the army to fight the Huns. He is old. She is young. She decides to go to the army instead of her father. Her challenge is to pass as a boy. This is difficult because she is not very strong like the other soldiers. But she is very clever. In their first battle, when she and her men face too many enemy soldiers, her idea saves them. <u>Mulan tells her men to make a big noise. The sound makes a wall of snow fall on the enemy soldiers.</u> Mulan and her men win the battle. This is the first of many times when Mulan makes a plan to save her men. The leader of the soldiers is very happy with Mulan for this and her secret is never discovered. Mulan succeeds in saving her father from fighting. Also, she brings honor to her family by being a good soldier.

Read the double underlined sentence. This is an example of how Mulan is clever. It <u>shows</u> us she is clever.

2 Read the paragraph about Ulysses. The author tells us that Ulysses is clever. But he doesn't <u>show</u> this idea.

On his journey home from fighting in the Trojan War, Ulysses faces many problems. In one story, he and his men get caught in the home of the Cyclops—a one-eyed monster. The Cyclops is very strong and very big, and he plans to eat Ulysses and his men. Ulysses must stop him. He does this by being very clever. He saves himself and his men, and they all return to their boats and sail for home.

Check (✓) the sentence that you think best shows that Ulysses is clever. Put a star in the paragraph where you think that sentence should go.

_____ **a.** His men want to run away from the monster with one eye, but he stays to fight him.

_____ **b.** He is afraid of the monster with one eye and tells his men to run away.

_____ **c.** Ulysses and his men dress up like sheep. The Cyclops thinks they are sheep, and they walk out and away.

_____ **d.** Ulysses is bigger and stronger than the Cyclops. He beats him in a fight.

3 Now go back to the first draft of your paragraph. Add supporting sentences that give specific examples and explanations to help explain main ideas.

GO TO MyEnglishLab FOR MORE SKILL PRACTICE.

EDIT: Writing the Final Draft

Go to MyEnglishLab and write the final draft of your hero paragraph. Carefully edit it for grammatical and mechanical errors such as spelling, capitalization, and punctuation. Make sure you use some of the vocabulary and grammar from the unit. Use the checklist to help you write your final draft. Then submit your paragraph to your teacher.

FINAL DRAFT CHECKLIST

❑ Does your paragraph describe a hero?

❑ Does it explain the hero's background, the challenge, how the hero overcame the challenge, and the result?

❑ Does it contain a topic sentence?

❑ Are there enough supporting sentences to explain the topic sentence?

❑ Do the supporting sentences give examples and explanations?

❑ Do you use time clauses in the present tense correctly?

❑ Do you use correct punctuation?

❑ Do you use new vocabulary that you learned in this unit?

UNIT PROJECT

Heroes are not just in stories. Sometimes real people can be heroes, and they can change the world:

- In the early 1800s in the United States, Harriet Tubman helped get slaves to freedom.
- Irena Sendler saved 2,500 Jewish children in Poland during World War II.
- In England in the early 1940s, Alan Turing developed the first computer.

Work in a small group. Write a paragraph describing a real-life hero, present or past. Follow these steps:

STEP 1: Locate a real-life hero

- Research real-life heroes online

STEP 2: Research the real-life hero

- Read about the hero online or from a book or magazine
- Take notes on your research

STEP 3: Write a paragraph of the real-life hero's story

- Does the hero leave his or her home on a journey?

- Does the hero face a challenge?

- Does the hero succeed?

- Does the hero return home a different person?

- Does the returning hero change his or her community?

STEP 4: Put each story in a class book called *Real-life Heroes.*

ALTERNATIVE WRITING TOPICS

Write about one of the topics. Use the vocabulary and grammar from the unit.

1. Write a paragraph about an old hero story from your culture. Think of Joseph Campbell's three parts to help you organize your writing.

2. According to Joseph Campbell, every culture has hero stories. There are many websites about everyday heroes, superheroes, and comic book heroes. Write a paragraph explaining why you think people are so interested in heroes and what heroes do for our lives?

3. Write a paragraph about your own hero story. Now that you know the important parts of any hero story, create your own hero and his or her story. Remember to start with the character in a setting and then tell the story of his or her journey.

■■■■■■■■■■■■■■■■■■■■■■■ *GO TO* MyEnglishLab *TO WRITE ABOUT ONE OF THE ALTERNATIVE TOPICS, WATCH A VIDEO ABOUT HEROES, AND TAKE THE UNIT 6 ACHIEVEMENT TEST.* ■■■■■■■■■■■■■■■■■■■■■■■

WHAT'S YOUR
Medicine?

1 FOCUS ON THE TOPIC

1. Describe the objects you see in the photo.

2. What do all of these objects have in common?

3. Has a doctor or helper ever used these objects to help you when you were sick?

GO TO MyEnglishLab TO CHECK WHAT YOU KNOW.

2 FOCUS ON READING

VOCABULARY

Today people have a lot of choice about who can help them when they are sick. They can see modern doctors or traditional healers. But many people choose to treat themselves at home when they have a common health problem.

1 Look at the pictures of several common health problems. Write the letter of the appropriate picture next to the name of the health problem.

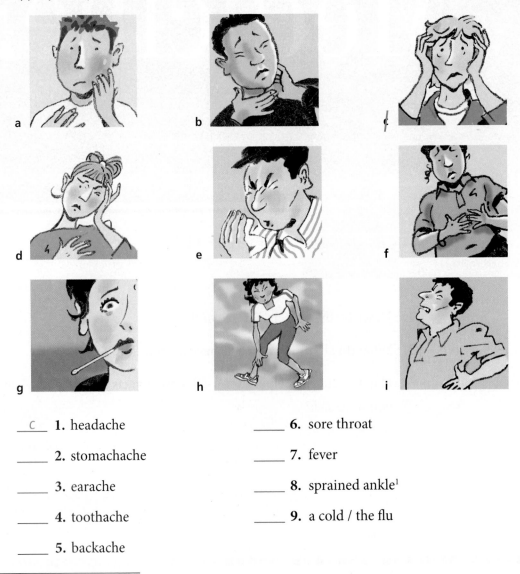

a

b

c

d

e

f

g

h

i

_c_ **1.** headache

_____ **2.** stomachache

_____ **3.** earache

_____ **4.** toothache

_____ **5.** backache

_____ **6.** sore throat

_____ **7.** fever

_____ **8.** sprained ankle[1]

_____ **9.** a cold / the flu

---

[1] **sprained ankle:** something you get when you fall and hurt your ankle but it's not broken

2 Read the list of words and their definitions.

blood: the red liquid that your heart pumps through your body

cure: to make a sick person well again

~~**fever:** when the body is sick and is hotter than normal~~

flow: when a liquid (water, for example) moves slowly from one place to another

patients: people who are getting medical treatment

popular: liked by many people

saliva: the liquid produced naturally in your mouth

sore throat: when the throat is red and painful

swelling: an area on your body that becomes larger than usual because of injury or sickness

swollen: bigger than usual because of injury or sickness

treat: to do something to a sick person to try to make him or her well again

veins: the tubes that bring blood back to the heart from the rest of the body

Now use the words from the list to complete the short descriptions of home remedies.

1. _____*Fever*_____: The most common remedy for this problem is cool water. Put the sick person in a cool bath or wash the person gently with a cool cloth. Don't put the person in ice water. It could be bad for him or her.

2. **Headache:** In China, some people _____ a headache with a coin (metal money). Hold the coin in your fingers and rub it back and forth across the forehead very hard. It will leave a red mark.

3. **Cold:** Some people believe you can _____ a cold by drinking a lot of orange juice. Orange juice has a lot of vitamin C. This helps the body fight illness.

4. _____: One remedy for this problem is honey. Eat one big spoonful three times a day. Most children love this remedy. The honey is sweet, and it feels nice on the throat. In fact, older _____ like it, too!

5. **Stomachache:** A _____ remedy is ginger (a spice from a light brown root). Cook 4 ounces of ginger in 1 quart of water for 1 hour. Drink a glass three times a day.

(continued on next page)

6. **Toothache:** When you have a toothache, everything that goes in your mouth hurts. Even the _____ in your mouth seems to hurt. For hundreds of years, the most common remedy for a toothache was to drink a glass of whiskey and have your neighbor pull out the tooth. These days, people just go to the dentist.

7. **Sprained ankle:** A sprained ankle often gets _____. To bring down the _____, do two things. First, put a bag of ice on the ankle. The cold makes the _____ in the ankle get smaller. Put the ice on the ankle for no longer than 10 minutes every couple of hours. Second, put your foot up high. This helps the _____ _____ back to the heart and makes the ankle go back to its normal size.

■■■ GO TO MyEnglishLab FOR MORE VOCABULARY PRACTICE.

PREVIEW

The following article is an excerpt from an encyclopedia entry. Read the title and the section headings. What kind of information do you think you will find in this article? Check (✓) the things you think you will find.

_____ **1.** how many kinds of leeches are in the world

_____ **2.** definition of *leech*

_____ **3.** how to catch leeches

_____ **4.** description of what leeches eat

_____ **5.** stories about people being leeched

_____ **6.** how leeches have been used in medicine in the past

_____ **7.** how leeches are used in medicine today

_____ **8.** how leeches will be used in medicine in the future

_____ **9.** why leeches are dangerous to use

Now read the whole article.

LEECH

1   **Biology**   Leeches are a kind of worm[1] from one millimeter to five centimeters long. They live all over the world. In general, leeches live in lakes and rivers. There are 650 kinds of leeches in the world. Only one kind is used in medicine. They are called medicinal leeches.

2   Medicinal leeches live on the **blood** of other animals. They have suckers[2] at both ends—one for feeding and one for holding on. Their **saliva** has three special chemicals that help them drink the blood. One is an anesthetic,[3] which allows the leech to feed without hurting the animal. The second chemical makes the **veins** open wide, and the third makes the blood **flow** from the veins for a long time.

3   A medicinal leech will drink 10 to 15 milliliters of blood at one time. This takes about 45 minutes. After the leech is full, it falls off. The bite will still bleed for another 24 hours because of the chemicals from the leech's saliva.

4   **History**   Leeches have been used in medicine for over 3,000 years. Leeches were most **popular** in Europe in the early 1800s. At this time, people thought that too much blood in a person's body made the person sick. Doctors put three or four leeches (or sometimes up to 50 or 60 leeches!) on a **patient's** body. The leeches took out the extra blood. Leeches were used to **cure** many illnesses, from **fevers** to broken legs.

5   Unfortunately, leeches often hurt more than they healed. For example, the Russian writer Nikolai Gogol was leeched because he had anemia, an illness caused by too *little* blood. He died a few days later. George Washington had a **sore throat**. He was leeched four times in two days. He too died a few days later. By the mid-1850s, people began to understand some of the problems with leeching, and it became unpopular.

6   **Today**   Today, doctors know more about leeches. They know when to use them and why. They understand that the chemicals in the leech saliva make leeches very useful in medicine. For this reason, the United States made it legal in 2004 to use leeches in reattachment surgeries.[4]

7   Until now, reattachment surgeries often failed. Take the example of a reattached finger. After surgery, the finger often becomes **swollen** with blood and the veins can't grow back together. The finger soon dies. Leeches take away this extra blood in two ways. One, they drink some of the blood from the finger. This only removes a spoonful of blood, however. The second way leeches remove this blood is the most important. Because of the chemicals in the leech saliva, the bite continues to bleed for hours and

---

[1] **worm:** a small snake-like animal that lives in the ground
[2] **suckers:** small round parts that connect the leech to the animal it feeds on
[3] **anesthetic:** a chemical that stops you from feeling pain
[4] **reattachment surgeries:** procedures performed when someone's finger or toe is cut off and the doctor puts it back on the hand or foot

(continued on next page)

hours after the leech falls off. With one or two leeches put on the finger twice a day for 4–5 days, the **swelling** completely goes away. With the swelling gone, the veins can grow back together and the finger lives. Doctors agree that leeches work better than anything else for this problem with reattachment surgeries.

8

There might be other medical uses for leeches too. For instance, some doctors have been able to reduce pain in patients with knee or elbow problems by **treating** them with leeches. The reason for this is not completely understood. But doctors think it has something to do with the chemicals in the leeches' saliva.

MAIN IDEAS

1 Look again at the Preview on page 162. How did your predictions help you understand the reading?

2 Circle the statement that best summarizes the main idea of each section of the article.

Biology

a. Leeches are worms that suck blood from other animals.

b. Leeches have suckers at both ends.

c. Leeches have both male and female parts.

History

a. People thought that too much blood caused illness. That's why leeches were popular.

b. Leeches killed George Washington and the Russian writer Nikolai Gogol.

c. Doctors treated every kind of illness with leeches. Often this caused a lot of problems.

Today

a. Many modern doctors use leeches to treat heart disease or knee and elbow pain.

b. Modern doctors are afraid that leeching will become popular again.

c. Modern medicine is finding that leeches are useful in reattachment surgeries.

DETAILS

These statements are false. Cross out the incorrect word and replace it with the correct word to make the statement true.

lakes

1. Leeches live in ~~oceans~~ and rivers all over the world.

2. A leech bite will still bleed for 12 hours after the leech falls off.

3. Leeches were most popular in Europe in the late 1800s.

4. The United States made it legal to use leeches for reattachment surgeries in 2001.

5. Today, people think sickness comes from too much blood.

6. Leeches increase swelling after reattachment surgeries.

7. Doctors disagree that leeches are the best thing to stop swelling after reattachment surgeries.

8. It takes a leech 24 minutes to feed and fall off.

MAKE INFERENCES

INFERRING JUDGMENTS

An **inference** is an educated guess about something that is not directly stated in the text. Readers often use inferences to make **judgments** about the information in a text. They make their inferences based on clues or specific pieces of information in the text.

Look at the example.

Based on clues in the text, infer how effective you think leeches are for treating some ailments. *Not effective=NE, Maybe effective=ME, Effective=E.* Then give the clues that helped you make your inference.

AILMENT	HOW EFFECTIVE IS LEECHING?	CLUES IN THE TEXT TO HELP YOU MAKE THE INFERENCE
anemia	NE	Paragraph 5: Anemia means very little blood. Gogol was anemic and died when they leeched him.

Fill out the chart by inferring how effective you think leeches are for treating certain ailments.

AILMENT	HOW EFFECTIVE IS LEECHING?	CLUES IN THE TEXT TO HELP YOU MAKE THE INFERENCE
1. BROKEN LEG		
2. FEVER		
3. FINGER REATTACHMENT		
4. KNEE PAIN		
5. SORE THROAT		

EXPRESS OPINIONS

Discuss the questions below with a partner. Give your opinions. Then share your answers with the class.

1. Imagine your doctor explained that the only way to save your toe after reattachment surgery was to have leeches on it for three days. Based on what you read, would you agree to do it or not? Explain.

2. Leeching was popular in the early 1800s. People understood that it worked sometimes. Because they didn't understand everything about leeching, they often used it when it didn't help. Do you think it's possible that today we are doing something similar? Can you think of a treatment or cure that we may use more than we should? Explain your thinking.

   Examples: medicine for children's classroom behavior problems

   medicine for depression (feeling sad all the time)

   medicine for losing weight

   Other ideas: _____

   _____

   _____

■■■■■■■■■■■■■■■■■■■■■■■■■■■ *GO TO* MyEnglishLab *TO GIVE YOUR OPINION ABOUT ANOTHER QUESTION.*

READING TWO GROSS MEDICINE

READ

1 Look at the boldfaced words and phrases in the reading and think about these questions:

1. Which words do you know the meaning of?

2. Can you use any of these words in a sentence?

2 Now read the story. It describes one man's experience with a traditional African doctor.

GROSS[1] MEDICINE

By Shetal Shah

1 I was trying to lie still and close my eyes. But I had to look.

2 They looked brown like chocolates. In fact, they were dark-green. But these "chocolates" were leeches. They were sucking out the pus[2] from my ankle. They were looking for blood.

3 This happened to me last summer when I rode my bicycle across Botswana, Africa. One day, I fell off my bike and got a small cut on my ankle. I forgot to wash the cut or put a **bandage** on it.

4 Three days later, I couldn't put on my shoe because my foot was so swollen. The pain in my ankle was terrible. And it was moving up my leg. I needed to find a doctor fast. But in Botswana, near the Kalahari Desert, a trip to the hospital looked like this: one day by car, three days by bicycle, or six days by donkey. This is when I met Ntemidisang and the leeches.

5 Ntemidisang was a traditional doctor from a village four kilometers away. He looked at the cut. He pushed on it carefully. Then he put his hand on my forehead and nodded[3] his head. Yes, I had a fever. He said he had to take the pus out of the ankle before I could bicycle to the city the next day to get some **antibiotics**.

6 Ntemidisang smiled to help me **relax**. He put a wet cloth on my forehead and opened a small metal box. Inside this dirty little box were the leeches.

7 I put my head back and watched the stars. I tried to think of other things. But I felt something cool on my skin. Ntemidisang put the leeches **gently** around the cut on my ankle. Suddenly, I felt them bite, and then I didn't feel anything.

8 Ntemidisang tried to make me laugh and forget about what was happening on my ankle. He wasn't funny, but I laughed.

9 An hour later, my ankle was bandaged and Ntemidisang was smiling. I was smiling too. I thanked him for helping me, and we said goodbye. Two days later, after riding 240 kilometers to the next city, I found a hospital. As the doctor was giving me a **shot** of antibiotics, I was thinking, "I sure don't like shots, but at least they aren't as gross as leeches!"

---

[1] **gross:** very unpleasant to look at or think about

[2] **sucking out the pus:** drinking the yellowish liquid from the dirty cut

[3] **nodded:** moved his head up and down to say "yes"

COMPREHENSION

Circle the best answer to complete each statement.

1. Shah was traveling through _____ when he fell off his bike.

    a. a village

    b. Botswana

    c. the mountains

2. Shah's ankle was swollen because _____.

    a. the leeches bit him

    b. he rode his bicycle too far

    c. he cut his ankle and didn't wash or bandage it

3. Shah needed a hospital. He couldn't get to one soon enough because

    _____.

    a. he didn't have a donkey

    b. it would take too long on his bicycle

    c. his car was too slow

4. Ntemidisang tried to make Shah laugh. He _____.

    a. wanted Shah to stop thinking about the leeches on his ankle

    b. wanted Shah to like him and think he was funny

    c. was nervous and didn't know what to do while they waited

5. The leeches helped Shah because they _____.

    a. cured him by healing the infection in his ankle

    b. took away the swelling so he could bike to the hospital

    c. made him relax

GO TO MyEnglishLab *FOR MORE VOCABULARY PRACTICE.*

READING SKILL

1 Read paragraphs 1 and 2 of Reading Two again. What does the text say and what is your reaction? What is the best way to interact with the text?

INTERACTING WITH THE TEXT: DOUBLE ENTRY NOTES

Strong readers are always **interacting with the text**. They read a sentence, have a thought or a question or a reaction to that sentence, and then go on to read another sentence that makes more thoughts, questions, and reactions. This interaction is important for deep understanding. When readings are difficult, students interact less. **Double entry note-taking** can help readers interact more with the text.

Look at the example and read the explanation.

Read the "double entry notes" made by a student. On the right, she wrote her thoughts or opinions about the text. On the left, she wrote short descriptions of what is stated in the text.

FACT	TEXT	THOUGHT/OPINION
It was difficult for him to lie still.	I was trying to lie still and close my eyes. But I had to look.	Oh, gross. This makes me feel sick. I don't ever want to have leeches on my body.
He had leeches put on his ankle. They were drinking his blood.	They looked brown like chocolates. In fact, they were dark-green. But these "chocolates" were leeches. They were sucking out the pus from my ankle. They were looking for blood.	He probably was annoyed at the traditional doctor.

Double entry note-taking allows you to interact with the reading more deeply. It gives you a structured way to ask questions, have opinions, or react to a reading at the same time that you understand the details of the text.

2 Read each excerpt from Reading Two and then write a "double entry note." On the right side, write your thoughts or opinions about the excerpt. On the left, write a summary of what is stated.

1.

FACT	TEXT	THOUGHT/OPINION
	Three days later, I couldn't put on my shoe because my foot was so swollen. The pain in my ankle was terrible. And it was moving up my leg. I needed to find a doctor fast. But in Botswana, near the Kalahari Desert, a trip to the hospital looked like this: one day by car, three days by bicycle, or six days by donkey. This is when I met Ntemidisang and the leeches.	

2.

FACT	TEXT	THOUGHT/OPINION
	I put my head back and watched the stars. I tried to think of other things. But I felt something cool on my skin. Ntemidisang put the leeches gently around the cut on my ankle. Suddenly, I felt them bite, and then I didn't feel anything. Ntemidisang tried to make me laugh and forget about what was happening on my ankle. He wasn't funny, but I laughed.	

1 Share your notes with a partner.

1. Compare your "fact" section: Did you write the same things? Do you agree that what you each wrote are facts?

2. Compare your "thought/opinion" section: Did you write the same things? Do you agree that what you each wrote is a thought or personal opinion?

GO TO MyEnglishLab FOR MORE SKILL PRACTICE.

STEP 1: Organize

Reading One (**R1**) gives lots of information about the science of leeches. Reading Two (**R2**) describes one patient's experience with leeches. Read the phrases based on Readings One and Two. Then write each phrase in the correct box in the chart.

- A few put on for about an hour
- Put on until they fall off once or twice a day for 4–5 days
- They suck out the pus from a dirty cut
- Make the blood flow
- Make the veins open wide
- ~~Include an anesthetic~~

	THE ENCYCLOPEDIA ENTRY (R1)	SHETAL SHAH'S EXPERIENCE (R2)
1. HOW DO LEECHES WORK?	Chemicals in the saliva: a. *include an anesthetic* b. c.	
2. HOW ARE THEY USED?		a. The doctor used them to take away the swelling from a bad cut. b.

Shetal Shah told the doctor he saw at the hospital about his experience with the leeches. The doctor laughed and said he was lucky. Leeches are good medicine. Because this doctor spoke English, Shetal Shah could ask him some questions he had about being leeched.

Complete the conversation between Shetal Shah and the doctor. Use information from the chart in Step 1.

SHETAL SHAH: I was nervous it would hurt when he put the leeches on. It didn't. Why not?

DOCTOR: _____

_____

SHETAL SHAH: Why did the bite keep bleeding so long afterward?

DOCTOR: _____

_____

GO TO MyEnglishLab *TO CHECK WHAT YOU LEARNED.*

VOCABULARY

REVIEW

1 Match the statements or questions on the left with the responses on the right.

_d_ **1.** Yoga is so **popular** these days.

____ **2.** You get headaches a lot. How do you **treat** them?

____ **3.** Do you think I have a **fever**?

____ **4.** Oh, I have a terrible **sore throat**.

____ **5.** Let's move her as **gently** as possible.

____ **6.** You need to get some **antibiotics** for that cut.

____ **7.** How can I bring down the **swelling** in my knee?

a. No, your forehead doesn't feel hot to me.

b. I drink a big glass of water and lie down in a dark room for an hour. It works most of the time.

c. Yeah, I guess you're right. It's all red and painful.

d. I know. Everyone I know is taking classes. We all want to be healthy, I guess.

e. Would some tea with honey make it feel better?

f. Yeah, it looks like her leg is broken so we don't want to bump it or be too rough.

g. Put a bag of frozen peas on it for 20 minutes. That should help.

2 Complete the sentences with the words from the box. Use one word more than once.

bandage	cure	patients	saliva	swollen
blood	flows	relax	shots	vein

1. I need a new _____bandage_____ for this burn on my hand. My old one got wet when I washed the dishes, and I should have a dry one.

2. Some people are very afraid of getting _____ when they go to see a doctor. One friend of mine asked me to go with her to hold her hand to help her _____!

3. Sometimes when you need a blood test, the nurse has trouble finding your _____. This often leaves a black-and-blue mark on your arm.

4. When you are hungry, your body makes extra _____ in your mouth. It's getting ready for the food that should soon be coming!

5. The Hudson River in New York _____ into the Atlantic Ocean.

6. I fell down the stairs yesterday. Today my ankle is so _____ I can't put on my shoe!

7. The doctors said they could _____ him if he took the medicine now. If he waited, they gave him six months to live.

8. Today in the United States, doctors are tired. They see twice as many _____ in a day as doctors did 25 years ago.

9. Most hospitals have something called a _____ bank. This is a place where they keep extra _____ for people who lose too much of their own when they have an accident or a long surgery.

Read each sentence. Circle the word or phrase that best matches the boldfaced word.

1. Last summer, I got a piece of glass in my foot. My wife washed my foot and pulled out the glass **gently**.

   a. in a way that was not hard

   b. in a way that was fast

2. If you get a bad cut, you must put a bandage on it right away. Hold the bandage to the cut **firmly**. This will stop the bleeding.

   a. in a soft way

   b. in a hard way

3. The four-year-old girl would not stop screaming. But the doctor talked to her **calmly**, and she finally sat still and listened.

   a. with a gentle, quiet voice

   b. with a loud, angry voice

4. Last summer, I broke my finger. I went to the hospital. I waited **patiently** for two hours. But after four hours, I was angry. Why did it have to take so long?

   a. becoming upset or mad

   b. without becoming upset or mad

5. The first time I met my husband's mother, I was surprised. He had told me she was not very nice and never smiled. But, instead, she greeted me **warmly** and made me feel very welcome.

   a. in a friendly way

   b. in an unfriendly way

6. He was a new doctor, so he put the bandage on **roughly**. The patient cried "Ouch!"

   a. in a soft way

   b. in a hard way

CREATE

Complete the conversation between the first-aid teacher and a student. Use as many of the words in parentheses as you can.

TEACHER: So, to review, what do you do if someone gets a sprained ankle?

STUDENT: _____
(bandage / patient / gently / swelling / swollen)

_____

_____

TEACHER: Good. Now tell me what you do when you see someone bleeding?

STUDENT: _____
(blood / veins / flow / patient / treat / firmly)

_____

_____

TEACHER: _____?
(sore throat / fever)

STUDENT: _____
(cure / popular / antibiotics)

_____

■■■■■■■■■■■■■■■■■■■■■■■■■■■■■■■■■■■ GO TO MyEnglishLab FOR MORE VOCABULARY PRACTICE.

GRAMMAR

1 Read the excerpt from Reading Two. Then answer the questions.

> Ntemidisang was a traditional doctor from a village four kilometers away. He looked at the cut. He pushed on it carefully.

1. How does the doctor push on Shetal's cut?

2. How do you know?

ADVERBS OF MANNER

1. **Adverbs of manner** describe action verbs. They say *how* or in what manner something happens. They are helpful when writing descriptions.	The doctor listened **carefully**.
2. Adverbs of manner usually come **after** the main verb.	The patient **talked slowly**.
3. Most adverbs of manner are formed by adding *-ly* to the adjective.	careful careful**ly** slow slow**ly**
4. Some **adjectives** end in *-ly* and have no adverb form.	He was a **lonely** old man. She has a **friendly** neighbor.
5. Some **adverbs** have the same form as the adjective.	**hard** *(adj.):* The test was **hard**. **hard** *(adv.):* She worked **hard**. **fast** *(adj.):* He is a **fast** runner. **fast** *(adv.):* She ran **fast**.
6. The adverb for *good* is *well*. Careful! *Well* is also an adjective that means "in good health."	**Good** game! You played **well**.

2 Like leeches, maggots are a kind of worm-like animal, but, unlike leeches, maggots live on dead flesh.[1] Like leeches, maggots were used in the past to treat certain medical problems. Recently, doctors have started using maggots again when nothing else works.

Read the paragraph and circle the adverbs.

The patient lay quietly on her bed. She was not feeling well. As soon as the doctor arrived, the patient felt more uncomfortable. She looked nervously at what was in the doctor's hand—a small jar with hundreds of small, white, worm-like things. And they were moving. The doctor smiled warmly at the patient. The patient felt better. She remembered that the maggots in the doctor's jar were going to help her. Parts of her left leg were dead because of an infection.[2] The maggots were going to eat the dead parts and allow the rest of her leg to heal well. It wasn't very nice to think about, but it was the best choice she had to save her leg.

Now write the adjective form of the adverbs you circled.

1. _____   3. _____

2. _____   4. _____

---

[1] **flesh:** the soft part of the body of a person or animal

[2] **infection:** a disease or sickness

3 Complete each sentence with the adjective or adverb form of the word in parentheses.

1. Mrs. Ewing became _____*slowly*_____ weaker over the months of her illness.
   (slow)

2. If you take an aspirin, your headache will go away _____.
   (quick)

3. Please be _____. I don't want anyone to get hurt!
   (careful)

4. My doctor is so friendly and _____. You'll like her.
   (warm)

5. Alice's husband was _____ when Alice returned from the hospital. He'd
   (happy)

   missed her.

6. The nurse washed my cut _____. It almost didn't hurt.
   (gentle)

7. The baby came in the middle of a snowy night. We drove very _____ to
   (careful)

   the hospital, but we got there in time.

8. His cut was _____. It hurt a lot.
   (painful)

4 Answer each question. Use one or two adverbs from the box in your answer.

badly	easily	gently	painfully	quickly	slowly	well
carefully	fast	hard	patiently	quietly	suddenly	

1. How do you walk when you have a sprained ankle?

   _____

   _____

2. How do you want your doctor to talk to you?

   _____

   _____

3. How do you take off a bandage?

   _____

   _____

4. How do you clean a cut before you put a bandage on?

_____

_____

5. How do you talk to a small child who is crying?

_____

_____

■ ■ ■ ■ ■ ■ ■ ■ ■ ■ ■ ■ ■ ■ ■ GO TO MyEnglishLab FOR MORE GRAMMAR PRACTICE AND TO CHECK WHAT YOU KNOW.

FINAL WRITING TASK

In this unit, you read about people all over the world still using traditional medicine and home remedies. Do you have childhood memories of your parents or grandparents treating you with a home remedy? What happened?

You are going to *write a narrative paragraph about an experience you had with a home remedy.* First, you will describe when and where you had this experience, what your health problem was, and what remedy you (or a parent) chose. Then you will describe what happened and how it worked. Use the vocabulary and grammar from the unit.*

PREPARE TO WRITE: Brainstorming

Brainstorming is a helpful way to get ideas for your writing. In brainstorming, you think of as many ideas as possible about a topic. No ideas are bad or wrong. You can brainstorm alone or in a group.

Follow the steps.

1. As a class, **brainstorm** as many home remedies as you can. Write them on the board. Ask questions about the ones that are unfamiliar to you. (For examples of some home remedies, go back to Vocabulary Exercise 2 on pages 161 and 162.)

2. Choose one remedy that you want to write about. Make sure it is one you have experience with.

---

* For Alternative Writing Topics, see page 185. These topics can be used in place of the writing topic for this unit or as homework. The alternative topics relate to the theme of the unit but may not target the same grammar or rhetorical structures taught in the unit.

3. Make a **cluster diagram**:

   a. Write the remedy in the middle of a piece of paper.

   b. In the space around it, write any words you can think of that are related to your experience of the remedy: your health problem, the place where it happened, the people who were there, how the remedy felt or tasted, etc.

Example

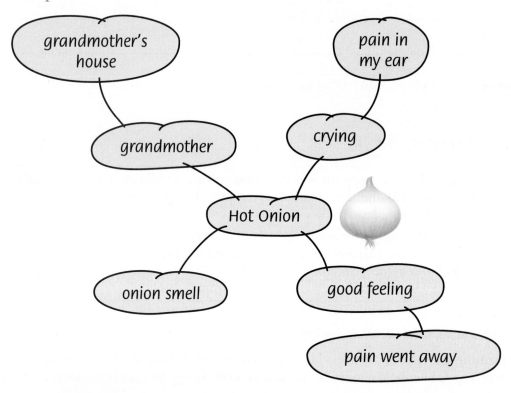

WRITE: A Narrative Paragraph

A **narrative** is a story about something that happened to you or someone else. It starts by telling *who* this story happened to, *when* it happened, and *where* it happened. Then it describes *what* happened and *how*.

1 Read the narrative paragraph. Then answer the questions.

When I was about six, I went to visit my grandmother in Canada. One day, I got a really bad earache. I was in a lot of pain, and I was crying. My grandmother said she knew what to do. First, she walked calmly to the kitchen cabinet and took out an onion. Then she cut it in half and put the two pieces in a pot of water. Next, she heated the onion in the water. Soon the smell of onion filled the kitchen. After that, she took out one half of the onion and put a small piece of cloth around it. Finally, she put the hot onion carefully against my ear. The heat from the onion felt very good on my ear. After a while, the pain went away.

Sally Collingsworth

Austin, Texas

1. **Who** is talking? _____

2. **When** did this happen? _____

3. **Where** did the story take place? _____

4. **What** was the health problem? _____

5. **What** was the remedy? _____

6. **Did** it work? _____

7. **How** did it work? _____

2 Now write the first draft of your narrative paragraph. Look at the diagram you made while brainstorming about your remedy. Use it to help you write a story describing one time when you used this remedy. You don't have to use every item you wrote in that diagram. But make sure you give the information needed to answer questions about **who**, **when**, **where**, **what**, and **how**.

REVISE: Using Time Order Words in a Narrative

When you tell a story in the first person, it helps the reader understand the story better if you describe what happened in **time order**—this means in the order in which things happened. We show time order by using time order words like these:

| First, . . . | Second, . . . | Then . . . | Next, . . . | After that, . . . | Finally, . . . |

1 Read the two stories. Which one is clearer (**A** or **B**)? Put a check (✓) next to it. Discuss your answer with a partner.

○ **A.**

When I grew up in Vietnam, all of us children frequently got head lice.[1] We didn't have chemicals or special shampoos to kill the lice. So my mother treated it the traditional way: with coconut[2] oil. My mother washed my hair with shampoo. I sat on a chair in front of her, and she combed out my hair slowly. This is one of my favorite memories as a kid: my mother singing to me while she combed my hair. I loved to close my eyes and listen to her rich voice. She poured some warm coconut oil carefully onto my hair. I loved this part. Usually we left the oil in for a few days. Mom shampooed and combed my hair one last time. My hair still looked oily, but the lice were gone.

---

[1] **head lice:** very small insects that live in human hair
[2] **coconut:** a very large brown nut; it is white inside and has liquid in the middle

○ **B.**

When I grew up in Vietnam, all of us children frequently got head lice. We didn't have chemicals or special shampoos to kill the lice. So my mother treated it the traditional way: with coconut oil. First, my mother washed my hair with shampoo. Then I sat on a chair in front of her and she combed my hair slowly. This is one of my favorite memories as a kid: my mother singing to me while she combed my hair. I loved to close my eyes and listen to her rich voice. After that, she poured some warm coconut oil carefully onto my hair. I loved this part. Usually we left the oil in for a few days. Finally, Mom shampooed and combed my hair one last time. My hair still looked oily, but the lice were gone.

Now read Story **B** again, and circle the time order words.

2 The following story would be clearer with some time order words. Fill in the blanks with the appropriate time order words from the box. Make sure you use proper punctuation and capitalization.

Finally, . . .   First, . . .   Next, . . .   Then, . . .

Last winter I had a bad cold. I was home from work for a week. I couldn't breathe well through my nose. I remembered an old remedy my grandmother used. _____ I put a towel over my head and put my head over the sink. _____ I turned on the hot water all the way. The towel was like a tent over the hot steamy water. _____ I breathed hard through my nose. I did this for about 15 minutes. _____ near the end, I could breathe more easily through one side of my nose. I did this three more times over the next 24 hours until I could breathe normally.

3 Now go back to the first draft of your narrative paragraph or story and add the time order words necessary to show in what order things happened.

GO TO MyEnglishLab FOR MORE SKILL PRACTICE.

EDIT: Writing the Final Draft

Go to MyEnglishLab and write the final draft of your paragraph. Carefully edit it for grammatical and mechanical errors, such as spelling, capitalization, and punctuation. Make sure you use some of the vocabulary and grammar from the unit. Use the checklist to help you write your final draft. Then submit your paragraph to your teacher.

FINAL DRAFT CHECKLIST

❑ Does your paragraph describe an experience you had with a home remedy?

❑ Does it answer the questions of *who, when, where, what,* and *how*?

❑ Does it describe what happened in time order?

❑ Do you use time order words correctly?

❑ Do you use adverbs of manner correctly?

❑ Do you use new vocabulary that you learned in this unit?

UNIT PROJECT

In this unit, you learned about traditional medicine from around the world. While these remedies may seem strange, many of them work well to cure common illnesses.

Compare health practices around the world. Follow these steps:

STEP 1: Work in a small group. Choose a common illness.

STEP 2: Research traditional ways of curing this illness. Interview people, look on the Internet, or find information at the library. How many different ways can you find to treat the same illness?

STEP 3: For each different way that you find, record the following information:

- What is the name of the illness?
- How common is the illness?
- What are some interesting facts and beliefs about the illness? What causes the illness? Who gets it?
- What medicine is used to treat this illness?
- What else is done to treat the illness?
- How long does it take to work?
- How successful is the treatment?

STEP 4: Write a summary of information.

STEP 5: Put the summaries of the whole class together to create a book that each student can take home.

ALTERNATIVE WRITING TOPICS

Write about one of the topics. Use the vocabulary and grammar from the unit.

1. In a letter to a friend, describe a strange or unusual medical treatment you (or someone you know) had. What was it? What was it for? Why was it strange or unusual? Would you (or the person who had it) agree to have it again?

2. Shetal Shah's description of his bike accident, hurt ankle, and the cure make a good story. In a paragraph or two, describe an accident you had. Where were you? What happened? How were you hurt? How did you heal?

3. Do you have a friend or family member who is a nurse or doctor? Write a paragraph or two describing why that person chose to work in medicine. Describe the person's job.

■■■■■■■■■■■■■■■■■■■■■■■■■ GO TO MyEnglishLab TO WRITE ABOUT ONE OF THE ALTERNATIVE TOPICS, WATCH A VIDEO ABOUT HEALTH PROBLEMS, AND TAKE THE UNIT 7 ACHIEVEMENT TEST. ■■■■■■■■■■■■■

ENDANGERED
Cultures

1 FOCUS ON THE TOPIC

1. What modern things do you see in the photo? What traditional things do you see in the photo?

2. Indigenous people are people whose families and cultures have been in one place for a very long time. Is the man from an indigenous or modern culture? Why do you think so?

3. What are some indigenous cultures you know about? What is happening to them today?

GO TO MyEnglishLab *TO CHECK WHAT YOU KNOW.*

READING ONE WILL INDIGENOUS CULTURES SURVIVE?

VOCABULARY

1 There are about 5,000 indigenous cultures in the world today. This map lists a few of them. The names in boldface refer to the indigenous cultures mentioned in this unit.

* Not alive today.

Study the map and read about some indigenous cultures today. Try to understand the boldfaced words in the list without looking them up in a dictionary.

Indigenous Cultures Today

1. Many indigenous cultures have disappeared; almost all indigenous cultures today are

    endangered, or in danger of disappearing.

2. The *Lutrawita* people of Tasmania, Australia, did not **survive** into the twentieth century. The last

    Lutrawita died in 1876. Most of them died between 1803 and 1833.

3. A long time ago, when the sea was lower, a land bridge connected Siberia and Alaska. The *Chukchi* people of Siberia and the *Inuit* people of Alaska were one culture. As the sea rose, it divided the land and the cultures. The *Chukchi* and *Inuit* are different today, but they share the same **roots**.

4. Like many indigenous tribes, the *Kogi* people have great respect for the earth. They believe the Gonawindua Mountain in Colombia is a **holy** place.

5. The *San* of southern Africa do not **adapt** well to modern life. Life in the desert is a very important part of their culture. If they move to towns and live in buildings, they become sick and sometimes die.

6. The *Al Murrah* people are from southern Arabia. Like all **nomadic** groups, they don't live in one place. The Al Murrah travel about 1,800 miles (3,000 kilometers) each year.

7. Some scientists think that the New Zealand *Maori* men and women have different **ancestors**. The ancestors of the men are from Melanesia and those of the women are from Taiwan. The scientists believe that 6,000 years ago, a group of women from Taiwan came in boats to Melanesia. At that point, some Melanesian men joined these women, and together they came to New Zealand and stayed.

8. The old ways of life for the *Mbuti* of the Democratic Republic of Congo are in danger. Large mining companies[1] are **destroying** the forest where the Mbuti live. The trees and the animals are disappearing and the water is bad.

9. The *Piraha* people of the Amazon have a **unique** language. It is unlike any other language in the world. It has no words for colors or numbers greater than two.

---

[1] **mining companies:** companies that take metals like gold and minerals like diamonds from the land

2 Match the words on the left with their definitions on the right.

_c_ 1. survive

_____ 2. roots

_____ 3. holy

_____ 4. adapt

_____ 5. nomadic

_____ 6. ancestors

_____ 7. destroy

_____ 8. unique

_____ 9. endangered

a. the beginning or origin of something; the connection with a place

b. unusual, the only one of its type

~~**c.** to continue to live in spite of difficulties or illness~~

d. members of your family who lived a long time ago

e. to change your behavior or ideas to fit a new situation

f. traveling from place to place

g. connected to a god and religion

h. at risk of disappearing

i. to damage something so badly that it cannot be fixed

■■■■■■■■■■■■■■■■■■■■■■■■■■■■■■■■■■■■■■ *GO TO* MyEnglishLab *FOR MORE VOCABULARY PRACTICE.*

PREVIEW

Before you read, look at the title of the magazine article. Why is it difficult for indigenous cultures to survive? Write three reasons you think the article might mention.

_____ .

_____ .

_____ .

Now read the article, "Will Indigenous Cultures Survive?"

WILL INDIGENOUS CULTURES SURVIVE?
By Alex Knight

1   In northern Colombia, a four-year-old *Kogi* Indian is carried into the Sierra Nevada mountains. He will live in a small dark house for 18 years. There he will learn to be a **holy** man. In the Amazon, a *Waorani* hunter follows animals by their smell. A *Mazatec* farmer in Mexico talks to other Mazatec by whistling[1] across the valleys. These stories come from three different indigenous cultures.

2   About 370 million people, or 5 percent of the world's population, belong to indigenous cultures. These cultures have deep **roots** in their histories, languages, and the places they live. Most of these cultures have lived the same way for thousands of years.

3   Change is an important part of any living culture. To **survive**, most indigenous cultures are learning to change in small ways. These small changes help them live with the bigger changes happening in the larger world. However, recent changes in the world are too big and are happening too fast. Most indigenous cultures can no longer **adapt** to them. For example, in Brazil, a gold rush[2]

brought diseases to the *Yanomami* in the 1990s. Now one-quarter of them are dead. In Ecuador, the *Cofan* homeland is full of chemicals from oil companies. The Cofan can no longer drink the water or grow food there. In India, over 250,000 indigenous people had to leave their homes in the Narmada River valley because the government built a dam[3] on the river.

4   What happens to the people from these cultures? Where do they go? Usually they have to move away from the lands of their **ancestors**. Often they move to the poor areas outside of large cities. They have to learn a new way of living and thinking. Their children will know little about the culture they came from.

5   There are about 4,000 cultures with their own **unique** languages alive today. Some scientists predict that by 2100, 90 percent of these will disappear. When a language disappears, the voice of a culture disappears. There are many indigenous people who are working hard to stop this from happening to their culture. They are fighting against governments who want them to become part of the modern world. They are fighting against oil and logging companies[4] who want their land.

6   The *Ariaal*, an indigenous **nomadic** group in Kenya, have been fighting for years. So far, their culture is surviving. The Ariaal understand that some changes may help them, but other changes may **destroy** their way of life. The Ariaal are trying to

(continued on next page)

---

[1] **whistling:** making a high or musical sound by blowing air out through your lips

[2] **gold rush:** a time when many people move to one area to look for gold

[3] **dam:** a wall built across a river to make a lake and produce electricity

[4] **logging companies:** companies that cut down trees to make wood and paper

stop the things that will hurt their culture and accept the helpful parts of the modern world. For example, the Kenyan government wants the Ariaal to move to villages. The government wants the Ariaal and other indigenous people to become more modern. The Ariaal know that if they move to villages, their nomadic way of life will disappear. So they aren't moving to villages. But many Ariaal are sending their children to Kenyan schools. They decided that schools are modern things that can help their culture survive.

7   There are no easy ways to save **endangered** indigenous cultures. We now know that indigenous cultures must adapt to survive. Most importantly, they must choose *how* they will adapt, as the Ariaal are trying to do. The big question is: Will the rest of the world let them?

MAIN IDEAS

1 Look again at the Preview on page 190. How did your predictions help you understand the article?

2 Circle the answer that best completes each main idea from the article.

1. Most indigenous cultures _____.

   a. are changing with modern times

   b. live the way they lived for thousands of years

2. Indigenous cultures are disappearing because _____.

   a. big changes are happening too fast

   b. their governments don't want them to adapt to the modern world

3. Indigenous cultures are fighting against _____ to keep their cultures.

   a. governments and big businesses

   b. other indigenous cultures

4. In order to survive, indigenous cultures must _____.

   a. listen to their governments

   b. decide how to adapt

5. For indigenous cultures to survive, the rest of the world must let them

   _____.

   a. have schools

   b. choose how to change

DETAILS

The article gives many examples to support general ideas. List the examples below each statement.

1. Three examples of the ways indigenous cultures understand the world and live their lives:

   a. *The Kogi Indian child goes to live in a dark house for 18 years.*

   b. _____

   _____

   _____

   c. _____

   _____

   _____

2. Three examples of changes that indigenous cultures cannot adapt to, and their results:

   a. _____ (*result:* _____)

   b. _____ (*result:* _____)

   c. _____ (*result:* _____)

3. One example of an indigenous group that is fighting to keep its culture:

   _____

4. One example of something that will hurt the Ariaal way of life:

   _____

5. One example of something from modern Kenyan culture that the Ariaal want:

   _____

MAKE INFERENCES

INFERRING THE AUTHOR'S ATTITUDE

An **inference** is an educated guess about something that is not directly stated in the text. Sometimes a text suggests the **author's attitude** (how he feels) about the subject he is writing about. Readers can infer the author's attitude from certain words and phrases he uses. These words and phrases make you think of particular feelings.

Look at the example and read the explanation.

- "They have to learn a new way of living and thinking. Their children will know little about the culture they came from." *(paragraph 4)*

Which words or phrases suggest the author's attitude?

a. *have to*

b. *their children will know little*

Have to tells us it is not the indigenous people's choice to learn new ways. Others are making them change. The author seems sad that indigenous people do not have a choice about how much they follow their history.

Their children will know little also tells us the author is sad. Everybody wants the children to know where they come from, and it is sad if they do not know their roots. He is also afraid that indigenous peoples' history will be forgotten. If the children do not learn it, no one will be able to pass it along.

After reading the text closely, especially certain words and phrases, we can **infer** the author's attitude about the situation indigenous people find themselves in: He feels bad about it; he isn't hopeful that it will get better.

Answer the questions.

1. In paragraph 4, sentences 1–4, which words and phrases help you infer the author's attitude about indigenous people leaving their ancestors' land?

   a. _____

   b. _____

2. In paragraph 5, sentences 1–3, which words and phrases help you infer the author's attitude about languages?

   a. _____

   b. _____

Now, with a partner, discuss what the author's attitude is about each topic and how the words and phrases help you understand his attitude.

EXPRESS OPINIONS

Discuss the questions below in a small group. Give your opinions. Then share your answers with the class.

1. The author names several things about the modern world (for example, dams, oil companies) that are hurting indigenous cultures. What are the benefits to these things? Do you think modern practices such as dam building and oil drilling should stop? Explain your answer.

2. Should governments try to help indigenous people survive? If so, what can they do?

■■■■■■■■■■■■■■■■■■■■■■■ *GO TO* MyEnglishLab *TO GIVE YOUR OPINION ABOUT ANOTHER QUESTION.*

READING TWO THE PENAN

READ

1 Look at the boldfaced words and phrases in the reading and think about the questions.

1. Which words do you know the meaning of?

2. Can you use any of these words in a sentence?

2 Now read the article about a visit to an indigenous people from Malaysia: the Penan.

THE PENAN:
PEOPLE OF THE FOREST━━━

*The Penan are an indigenous nomadic culture in Malaysia. The following journal is from a visit to the Penan from a few years ago. It describes the Penan connection to their forest home that is still very true today. Three hundred Penan nomads still live in the forest. Visitors to the area find the **settled** Penan are also still deeply **connected** to their nomadic traditions, and they are continuing to fight to save their forest home. The companies and projects they **protest** are always changing, but what they fight for remains the same: They fight to keep their culture alive.*

(continued on next page)

1   I am going back to visit my Penan friends after 10 years. The big ships[1] are the first things I see as I turn my boat to go up the river. They are waiting to get filled up with logs[2] from the forests where the Penan live.

2   When I arrive at the Penan village of Long Iman, my old friend, Tu'o, greets me warmly. Tu'o was born a nomad. But 30 years ago, the Malaysian government **convinced** Tu'o to move to Long Iman. The government said that it was better for the Penan to live in villages and become part of modern Malaysia. But they also wanted to sell the forest to the logging companies. Since that time, thousands more Penan have moved to villages. The Penan fought to keep their home in the forest, but the logging companies were too **powerful**.

3   Long Iman is a sad place. The river is dirty, and there is mud[3] everywhere. In the evening, children watch television, but they don't understand the language. Tu'o says he is sorry about the small amount of food at dinner. "How can you feed your guests[4] in a village? It's not like the forest where there is a lot of food. In the forest, I can give you as much as you want. Here, you just sit and look at your guests, and you can't give them anything. My house here is strong, and we have beds and pillows. But you can't eat a pillow."

4   I am here to find one of the last groups of Penan nomads. There are only about 300 Penan nomads left. The group I am looking for now lives in the Gunung Mulu National Park, where the forest is safe from logging companies. Tu'o says he will take me to them. We leave the next morning. After three days of traveling, we reach the nomads.

5   Asik, the leader, welcomes us. In the evening, we eat with the nomads. We eat baskets of beautiful fruit, mushroom soup, delicious vegetables, and two pigs—all collected or caught in the forest. Sharing is an important part of the Penan's way of life. They do not even have a word for "thank you."

6   I ask Asik about the villages like Long Iman. He says, "There are no more trees, and all the land is no good. The animals are gone; the river is muddy. Here we sleep on hard logs, but we have plenty to eat."

---

[1] **ships:** large boats

[2] **logs:** trees that have been cut down to be used for wood

[3] **mud:** dirt and water mixed together

[4] **guests:** people you invite to your house to visit or share a meal

COMPREHENSION

Circle the answer that best completes each statement. Then discuss your answers with a partner.

1. The number of nomadic Penan in the forest is _____.

   a. increasing

   b. staying the same

   c. decreasing

2. One reason the forest is disappearing is _____.

   a. the Penan are burning it

   b. the government is building villages

   c. the logging companies are cutting it down

3. _____ Long Iman.

   a. Tu'o was born in

   b. The government asked Tu'o to move to

   c. Tu'o decided by himself to move to

4. Tu'o is sorry he doesn't have more _____.

   a. boats for the river

   b. food for his guests

   c. children to help him

5. The nomadic Penan are happy because they have _____.

   a. lots of food

   b. lots of logs

   c. a muddy river

■■■■■■■■■■■■■■■■■■■■■■■■■■■■■ GO TO MyEnglishLab FOR MORE VOCABULARY PRACTICE.

READING SKILL

1 Read paragraphs 2 and 3 of Reading Two again. Notice the two different ways the author tells about Tu'o talking.

UNDERSTANDING THE PURPOSE OF QUOTED SPEECH

When telling a story, writers use direct **quotes** to help the reader "hear" the people in the story and understand them better.

Look at the examples and read the explanations.

- My old friend, Tu'o, greets me warmly. *(paragraph 2)*

The reader **cannot hear** what Tu'o says here. He is just a person in the village, and we know that he is "warm," but we don't know much more about him.

- Tu'o says . . . "How can you feed your guests in a village? It's not like the forest where there is a lot of food. In the forest, I can give you as much as you want. Here, you just sit and look at your guests, and you can't give them anything. My house here is strong, and we have beds and pillows. But you can't eat a pillow." *(paragraph 3)*

The reader **hears** Tu'o, here. We hear his apology. We hear him remember the forest, and we can hear how he feels in the forest. We also hear that, although he is sad in the village, he is still a little bit funny. (He makes a joke about eating a pillow.)

2 Work with a partner. Read paragraphs 5 and 6 again. Underline the sentences that refer to Asik speaking. Then write them on the lines. Which sentences tell you more about Asik?

1. **Paragraph 5:** _____

2. **Paragraph 6:** _____

_____

_____

GO TO MyEnglishLab *FOR MORE SKILL PRACTICE.*

STEP 1: Organize

Reading One is about indigenous cultures in general. Reading Two is about the Penan, an example of an indigenous group.

Look at the chart. Read each general statement from Reading One (**R1**) and decide how the Penan (**R2**) are an example of that general statement.

GENERAL STATEMENT (R1)	HOW ARE THE PENAN AN EXAMPLE? (R2)
1. "These cultures have deep roots in their histories, languages, and the places they live."	*The Penan eat fruit, vegetables, and meat—all caught in the forest.* *Sharing is an important part of Penan life.*
2. "Recent changes in the world are too big and are happening too fast. Most indigenous cultures can no longer adapt to them."	
3. "Oil and logging companies . . . want their land."	
4. "Usually they have to move away from the lands of their ancestors."	

STEP 2: Synthesize

Read the Web page and complete the letter on the next page, using information from the chart in Step 1.

Indigenous People UPDATE: The Penan

Logging companies, and now palm oil companies, have been destroying the Penan's forest since 1970. As the forests are logged, the rivers become muddy, and the fish die. The animals go farther and farther into the forest, and this makes life difficult for the Penan.

Now the Penan have another problem: The Malaysian government is building 12 new dams in Penan areas. If the next new dam gets built, 20,000 people, including many Penan, will have to move because their villages will be under water.

The Penan have been fighting back peacefully, but many Penan have been arrested.

What can you do?

Please write to the Chief Minister of Sarawak to help the Malaysian government understand the Penan.

Dear Chief Minister,

Please. It's very important that Malaysia support the Penan.

Like all indigenous cultures around the world, the Penan have deep roots in their histories, language, and the places where they live.

_____

_____

_____

This way of life is in danger.

_____

_____

_____

Because of these changes, the Penan can no longer live as they did for thousands of years.

_____

_____

_____

Most of them have to move away from the land of their ancestors.

_____

_____

_____

Sincerely,

_____
        (your name)

GO TO MyEnglishLab TO CHECK WHAT YOU LEARNED.

VOCABULARY

REVIEW

Read each group of sentences. Pay attention to the boldfaced words. Cross out the sentence that does not make sense. Discuss with a partner why it does not make sense.

1. a. ~~The people have lived in this town for 50 years. They are **nomadic**.~~

   b. Many indigenous people were **nomadic** in the past, but now most of them live in villages.

   c. **Nomadic** people usually move after their animals eat all of the food in one area.

2. a. American blues music has its **roots** in African American culture.

   b. Our house is very old. Its **roots** are from the 1800s.

   c. Most people who live in the United States have **roots** in other countries.

3. a. These cups are all handmade, so each one is **unique**.

   b. McDonald's hamburgers in New York are **unique** because they are just like the McDonald's hamburgers in Los Angeles.

   c. Claire spent a year looking for a wedding dress that was **unique**.

4. a. The backpacking trip through Nepal was tough, but I **survived**!

   b. Today people who have AIDS can **survive** for many years because we have new medicines.

   c. From the time I was eight years old until I went to university, I **survived** in Canada. Then I moved to the United States.

5. a. Your hair is fine the way it is. Don't **adapt** anything.

   b. The most difficult thing for Noriko to **adapt** to when she moved to England was the food.

   c. Several people got headaches on the first day of the trip to the mountains. But after a couple of days, their bodies **adapted** to being in such a high place.

(continued on next page)

6. **a.** Muslims all over the world fast (stop eating and drinking) during the days of the **holy** month of Ramadan.

   b. Tibetans believe that some mountains are **holy**—a god or spirit lives in these mountains.

   c. This office building must be a **holy** place on weekdays. I bet over 500 people work here every day.

7. **a.** Please don't touch the photo with your dirty hands. You'll **destroy** it.

   b. I had a small accident yesterday. I **destroyed** the car a little. I'm sure it can be fixed.

   c. In Sri Lanka in 2005, the hurricane **destroyed** thousands of homes.

8. **a.** Sssh! Speak quietly. You are too **powerful**.

   b. Big companies are often rich and **powerful**, so they get what they want.

   c. In 2011, a **powerful** group of people stopped a dam from being built in Peru.

9. **a.** We have moved three times this year. I don't feel very **settled**.

   b. In the United States, the indigenous people used to be nomadic, but now they are **settled** in places called reservations.

   c. I am tired of being **settled**. I want to go on vacation.

10. **a.** Assou **convinced** his father to buy a TV so that he could see programs from all over the world.

    b. Governments often **convince** new villages for indigenous people.

    c. I **convinced** my mother to visit me in the United States, but I never got her to speak any English.

11. **a.** My grandmother taught me Sami, so I have stayed **connected** to the Sami traditions.

    b. The logging companies are **connected** to the traditions of the places they work.

    c. I have many relatives in Nepal, but I have never met them. We are not **connected** at all.

12. **a.** Let's invite our **ancestors** to the wedding!

    b. My **ancestors** came to America from Germany in 1680.

    c. Most Cape Verdean people have Portuguese and African **ancestors**.

13. **a.** Aluo is an **endangered** language because most Yi people choose to speak Chinese now.

   b. Sumatran tigers are **endangered** because people have been killing them for years.

   c. Volkswagen Beetle cars from the 1970s must be **endangered** because I don't see them very often.

14. **a.** Sally and Ed don't get along very well. They always **protest** each other.

   b. Many people all over the world **protested** the Iraq war.

   c. If the schools stop teaching our indigenous language, I am going to **protest**.

EXPAND

A reporter is interviewing an indigenous people's leader. Match the questions with the responses below. Pay attention to the boldfaced words or phrases.

Questions

_b_ 1. Do you think you'll catch a lot of fish on your trip today?

____ 2. I thought this indigenous culture was against modern culture. Why is that man using a cell phone?

____ 3. What do you think of your young people who want to settle in the cities and leave the old ways?

____ 4. What do you think will help your people to survive?

____ 5. Why do all the women sit on one side and the men on the other?

____ 6. How many children from this village do you think will attend school in the fall?

Responses

a. I'm not sure. It's been our **custom** for so long.

b. I doubt it. I went out yesterday and didn't get anything.

c. I **expect** we'll get a large group. Maybe 15 to 20.

d. We hold onto our own culture very strongly. But frequently we will **adopt** a custom or tool that we find useful.

e. I think we must learn how to **stand up to** the governments and the companies that try to take away our lands.

f. Of course, this makes us sad. But if they want to **integrate** into modern culture, we can't stop them. We hope they will bring to the modern world all that they learned in our world.

CREATE

You are interviewing a leader of one of the indigenous groups mentioned in this unit. Complete the interview. Use at least nine words from the box. Use different types of questions.

adapt	convinced	expect	nomad	settled
adopt	custom	holy	nomadic	stand up to
ancestors	destroy	integrate	protest	survive
connected	doubt	leader	roots	unique

YOU: _What is the name of your culture?_ _____

LEADER: _____

YOU: _What are some of the customs of your culture?_ _____

LEADER: _____

_____

_____

YOU: _____

LEADER: _____

_____

_____

YOU: _____

LEADER: _____

_____

_____

■■■■■■■■■■■■■■■■■■■■■■■■■■■■■■■■■■ *GO TO* MyEnglishLab *FOR MORE VOCABULARY PRACTICE.*

GRAMMAR

1 Read about some Penan leaders' trip to the capital city. Underline the verbs that refer to the future.

Several Penan leaders are traveling to the capital city in three days to protest the Murum Dam project. They are going to ask the government officials to stop building the Murum Dam. They will tell them how difficult it will be for whole villages of Penan to move. One elder is giving a short speech to the Parliament. The members of Parliament will listen to him politely. But the Penan wonder, "Will anyone hear us? Will anyone stop the dam?" They hope so, but they are not sure.

Write an example of each of the three different forms used to talk about the future.

1. _____

2. _____

3. _____

EXPRESSING PREDICTIONS AND FUTURE PLANS

There are **different ways to talk about the future** in English.

1. Use *will* + **base form** of the verb for **predictions**.	They **will listen** to him politely, but they **won't do** anything.
	Will anything **change**? No, nothing **will change**.
Do not use *will* + base form of the verb for plans made before now.	INCORRECT: I can't go to the capital with you because I will get married.
2. Use *be going to* + **base form** of the verb for **predictions**.	They **are going to listen** to him politely, but they **are not going to do** anything. *(prediction)*
Use it also for **plans made before now**.	They **are going to ask** the officials not to build the dam. *(plan made before now)*
	Are they **going to meet** with the president?
3. Use the **present progressive** (*be* + *-ing* form of the verb) for **plans made before now**. Future time is indicated by future time words or by the context.	The leader **is giving** a short speech to the Parliament *next Tuesday*.
	When **are the leaders coming** back?
Do not use the present progressive to make predictions.	INCORRECT: The Penan are surviving in the future.

2 Complete the speeches by three Penan leaders. Use a future form of the verb in parentheses. For each blank, two forms are possible; choose one. Use each of the three ways of expressing the future at least once.

Speech 1. The government says that it is helping us. The logging companies say

that the Penan people _____will make_____ lots of money. But the jobs
                              1. (make)

_____ with the forest. When the forest is gone, there
        2. (disappear)

_____ any more jobs. Why do we need jobs anyway? My
        3. (not be)

grandfather didn't have a job. My father didn't have a job. They lived off the

forest. But there _____ any more forest to live off in a few
                          4. (not be)

years—for anyone.

Speech 2. My aunt moved to a government village 20 years ago. She says, "This logging

is like a big tree that fell on my chest. I wake up every night and talk with

my husband about the future of my children. I always ask myself, 'When

_____?'"
        5. (it / end)

My elderly grandmother went to live with that aunt a year ago, but she

_____ back to the forest. "I _____ soon,"
        6. (come)   7. (die)

she says. "I _____ in that government village. My spirit
                    8. (not die)

_____ there."
        9. (never rest)

Speech 3. We _____ your trucks pass. We need some answers. Soon
                  10. (not / let)

two dams _____ finished. The electricity company says they
                 11. (be)

_____ ten more dams before 2020. Twenty years ago you told
     12. (build)

us to move to villages. Now you tell us we must leave our villages. Where

_____ us? _____ us again in another 20 years? If
   13. (you / move)   14. (you / move)

these 12 dams are built, our ancestors' land _____ underwater.
                                                    15. (be)

Our history _____ underwater. How _____ their
                 16. (be)   17. (our children / know)

history if they cannot see the land?

3 Write six questions about the future of the Penan and other indigenous cultures. For
items **1–3**, use the words given. For items **4–6**, write your own questions. Make sure you
use appropriate forms.

1. Penan culture / disappear?

_____

2. How many / Penan nomads / be alive / in 50 years?

_____

3. anyone / speak Penan / in 100 years?

_____

4. _____

5. _____

6. _____

4 Work with a partner. Read the questions your partner wrote for Exercise 3. Then write answers to your partner's questions. Make sure you use appropriate forms for talking about the future.

1. _____

2. _____

3. _____

4. _____

5. _____

6. _____

■■■■■■■■■■■■■■■■ *GO TO* MyEnglishLab *FOR MORE GRAMMAR PRACTICE AND TO CHECK WHAT YOU LEARNED.*

FINAL WRITING TASK

In this unit, you read about endangered cultures in general and about one culture in particular, the Penan of Malaysia. Do you think the Penan will survive the next 100 years?

You are going to *write a paragraph to make a prediction about the survival of the Penan.* You will give reasons for your prediction. And you will support your reasons with facts from Reading One and Reading Two or any facts you know from your general knowledge. Use the vocabulary and grammar from the unit.*

PREPARE TO WRITE: Taking Notes from a Reading

Taking notes from a reading is an important tool for writing. To take useful notes, you must first decide what your opinion on the topic will be. Then go back to the reading and take notes on the **parts** that show that your opinion is the correct one. When you take notes, don't write in full sentences—use short phrases or one word.

---

* For Alternative Writing Topics, see page 215. These topics can be used in place of the writing topic for this unit or as homework. The alternative topics relate to the theme of the unit but may not target the same grammar or rhetorical structures taught in the unit.

1 Read the article about the Tarahumara culture. Do you think the Tarahumara will survive? What is your opinion?

The Feet Runners

1   The *Tarahumara* people live in the mountains of Mexico. The high mountains make it difficult to know how many Tarahumara are living today. But most people agree the number is close to 70,000.

2 The Tarahumara call themselves the *Raramuri*. This means "feet runners" or "those who walk well." In fact, they are known for being very strong runners. Because their villages are far apart, the Tarahumara run long distances all the time.

3 The Tarahumara have resisted[1] the modern world since the 1700s. They refuse to adapt to the changes of modern Mexico. They run away from change. Whenever an outside group gets too close, the Tarahumara move higher into the mountains. They want to keep their people and their culture away from modern Mexican culture. Many Tarahumara still dress, farm, and live like they did long ago. They teach their children to love their customs, their language, and their way of life.

4 The Tarahumara have survived 400 years since the Spanish first came to Mexico. But what about the next 400 years?

5 There have been many changes in the past 20 years. The Tarahumara live in the mountains called Copper Canyon. Gold and silver deep in the mountains of Copper Canyon are very interesting to mining companies. Also, logging companies are slowly destroying the forests of this area. These big companies will destroy the land and the water if they come to get the trees and the gold and silver. Tourism companies are building large hotels in the area, and that will certainly change the culture. Will the Tarahumara be able to survive? The world will have to wait and see.

---

[1]**resisted:** not allowed something to change

2 Imagine you believe the Tarahumara will survive. Check (✓) the notes that support your opinion.

> ___ known for being strong runners
>
> ___ have resisted modern Mexico since 1700s
>
> ___ call themselves Raramuri
>
> ___ still dress and farm like they did years ago
>
> ___ new people get too close, they move higher
>
> ___ live in Copper Canyon
>
> ___ 400 years of change have not killed them

3 Imagine you believe the Tarahumara will not survive. Go back to the reading and make two notes that support this opinion. Remember: Use short phrases.

NOTE 1: _____

_____

NOTE 2: _____

_____

4 Decide if you think the Penan will survive the next 100 years or not. Then read Readings One and Two again and take notes on the facts that show why your opinion is correct.

WRITE: A Paragraph Based on an Outline

To write a well-organized paragraph, you need to select the right information. Read the directions for your writing assignment carefully. They can often help you organize your ideas by telling you what information to include.

An **outline** is another useful tool for writing. An outline helps you organize your ideas before you start writing.

1 Read the outline about the Tarahumara.

Main idea *(prediction)* →

Reason 1 *(for prediction)* →

Facts *(from notes)* →
that support Reason 1 →

Reason 2 *(for prediction)* →

Facts *(from notes)* →
that support Reason 2 →

> **OUTLINE**
> **Will the Tarahumara survive?**
>
> The Tarahumara will not survive the next 100 years.
>
> **A.** Won't have any more land to run to
>   **1.** Every contact with modern world, they move higher up the mountain
>   **2.** If mining companies come in, they will destroy their land
>
> **B.** Refuse to adapt to change
>   **1.** They live today as they always have
>   **2.** Don't adapt, just run away

2 Read another outline on the Tarahumara. Complete the outline by choosing the best reasons for **A** and **B** from the lists below.

> **OUTLINE**
> **Will the Tarahumara survive?**
>
> The Tarahumara will survive the next 100 years.
>
> **A.** _____
>   **1.** Still dress, farm, live as did 400 years ago
>   **2.** Teach children to love customs and language
>
> **B.** _____
>   **1.** 70,000 living today

The Best Reason for A

1. They are interested in changing their culture.

2. They work hard to stop their culture from disappearing.

3. They haven't changed anything in their culture for 400 years.

The Best Reason for B

1. They have a small number of people.

2. They have a fairly large population.

3. We don't know exactly how many are living today.

3 Write an outline about your prediction for the Penan. Your prediction will be your main idea. Provide at least two or three reasons for your prediction. Use your notes for the facts that support your reasons.

4 Now write the first draft of your paragraph, based on your outline.

_____

_____

_____

_____

REVISE: Writing a Concluding Sentence

A **concluding sentence** can restate the main idea of a paragraph. In this case, for example, you can restate your prediction. A concluding sentence can also make a suggestion or express an opinion.

1 Read the paragraph. Then look at the three possible concluding sentences below. Decide what kind of conclusions these are. Write **R** (restates the main idea), **S** (makes a suggestion), or **O** (expresses an opinion) next to each.

> I predict that the Tarahumara will not survive the next 100 years. One reason is they won't have any more land to run to. They won't be able to move higher into the mountains every time modern people get too close to them. Also, if mining companies come in, they will destroy the mountains where the Tarahumara live. Another reason they will not survive is that they refuse to adapt to change. They dress and farm the same way they did 400 years ago. To survive, indigenous cultures must adapt. The Tarahumara have only run away. Soon, they won't be able to even do this.
>
> _____
>
> _____
>
> _____

Concluding Sentences

_____ **1.** This is why the Tarahumara will not survive another 100 years.

_____ **2.** In my opinion, if the Tarahumara can't adapt to change, they'll disappear forever.

_____ **3.** To save the Tarahumara, I think the Mexican government should stop the big companies from destroying the Tarahumara's land.

2 Read the paragraph. Write a concluding sentence. Share it with a partner.

I predict that the Tarahumara will survive the next 100 years. One reason is the Tarahumara work hard to hold onto their culture. They still dress and farm the same way they did 400 years ago. Also, they teach their children to love their customs and their language. Another reason is the Tarahumara have a fairly large population. There are about 70,000 Tarahumara living today.

_____

_____

_____

3 Now go back to the first draft of your paragraph and write a concluding sentence.

GO TO MyEnglishLab FOR MORE SKILL PRACTICE.

EDIT: Writing the Final Draft

Go to MyEnglishLab and write the final draft of your paragraph. Edit it carefully for grammatical and mechanical errors, such as spelling, capitalization, and punctuation. Make sure you use some of the vocabulary and grammar from the unit. Use the checklist to help you write your final draft. Then submit your paragraph to your teacher.

FINAL DRAFT CHECKLIST

❑ Does your paragraph clearly predict if the Penan will or will not survive the next 100 years?

❑ Does it give clear reasons for your prediction?

❑ Does it use facts from the readings or from your general knowledge to support your prediction?

❑ Do you use the proper verb tenses when making your prediction?

❑ Do you use the tenses correctly?

❑ Do you use a concluding sentence?

❑ Do you use new vocabulary that you learned in this unit?

UNIT PROJECT

Work in pairs. Research an endangered culture or people and prepare a one-page status report. Follow these steps:

STEP 1: Choose an endangered culture or people from the map on page 188.

STEP 2: Go to the Internet or to the library to do research about this group of people. Information to look for:

- name
- population
- location
- traditional customs
- reasons the culture is endangered
- predictions for these people

STEP 3: Prepare a one-page status report about this endangered culture or people. Use the following format. Feel free to add photos or other information that you find.

Status Report on _____

Population: _____

Location: _____

Traditional customs: _____

_____

Reasons the culture is endangered: _____

_____

My predictions for this culture: _____

_____

STEP 4: Share your report with the class.

ALTERNATIVE WRITING TOPICS

Write about one of the topics. Use the vocabulary and grammar from the unit.

1. Is it a good idea to try to save indigenous cultures? In a letter to an editor, explain why or why not. Give examples.

2. Some indigenous cultures have become modern cultures. In a paragraph or two, write about one of these cultures, and tell how it adapted. How different is that culture today from the way it was before?

3. Find someone who is from an indigenous culture. Ask him or her about that culture and write a paragraph or two about it. Write about how that culture thinks and lives. Be sure to use examples in your writing.

■■■■■■■■■■■■■■■■■■■■■■■■■■ *GO TO* MyEnglishLab *TO WRITE ABOUT ONE OF THE ALTERNATIVE TOPICS, WATCH A VIDEO ABOUT ENDANGERED CULTURES, AND TAKE THE UNIT 8 ACHIEVEMENT TEST.* ■■■■■■■■■■

GRAMMAR BOOK REFERENCES

Northstar: *Reading and Writing Level 2,* Fourth Edition	Focus on Grammar Level 2, Fourth Edition	Azar's Basic English Grammar, Fourth Edition
Unit 1 Descriptive Adjectives and Possessive Adjectives	**Unit 5** Descriptive Adjectives **Unit 12** Possessives: Nouns, Ajectives, Pronouns; Object Pronouns; Questions with Whose	**Chapter 14** Nouns and Modifiers: 14–1 **Chapter 6** Nouns and Pronouns: 6–3
Unit 2 Simple Past, Regular and Irregular	**Unit 3** Past of *Be:* Statements, *Yes/No* Questions; *Wh*-Questions **Unit 18** Simple Past: Affirmative and Negative Statements with Regular Verbs **Unit 19** Simple Past: Affirmative and Negative Statements with Irregular Verbs **Unit 20** Simple Past: *Yes/No* and *Wh*-Questions	**Chapter 8** Expressing Past Time, Part 1: 8–4, 8–6, 8–9, 8–10, 8–11 **Chapter 9** Expressing Past Time, Part 2: 9–4, 9–5, 9–6
Unit 3 Comparative Form of Adjectives	**Unit 33** The Comparative	**Chapter 15** Making Comparisons: 15–1, 15–2, 15–5, 15–6
Unit 4 Imperative Sentences	**Unit 7** Imperatives: Suggestions with *Let's, Why don't we . . . ?*	**Chapter 13** Modals, Part 2: Advice, Necessity, Requests, Suggestions: 13–6, 13–9

Northstar: *Reading and Writing Level 2,* Fourth Edition	Focus on Grammar Level 2, Fourth Edition	Azar's Basic English Grammar, Third Edition
Unit 5 *Too much / Too many / too +* adjective	**Unit 29** *Too much / Too many / Too +* Adjective	**Chapter 12** Modals, Part 1: Expressing Ability: 12–7
Unit 6 Time clauses in the present tense	Part VIII From Grammar to Writing: Time Clauses with *When*	**Chapter 9** Expressing Past Time, Part 2: 9–7, 9–8
Unit 7 Adverbs of Manner	**Unit 34** Adverbs of Manner	**Chapter 14** Nouns and Modifiers: 14–4
Unit 8 Expressing Predictions and Future Events	**Unit 24** *Be Going To* for the Future	**Chapter 10** Expressing Future Time, Part 1: 10–1

UNIT WORD LIST

The Unit Word List is a summary of key vocabulary from the Student Book. Words followed by an asterisk (*) are on the Academic Word List (AWL).

UNIT 1

advice
career
challenge (n.)*
experience (n.)
hire (v.)
ideal (adj.)
interview (n.)
manager
posting (n.)
résumé
reward (n.)
running your own business
salary
setting (n.)
skill
training (n.)

UNIT 2

combine (v.)
create*
curious
encourage
fact
focus on*
logical*
measure (v.)
original
piece (n.)
prove
solve
study (n.)
take a risk

UNIT 3

arrest (v.)
bill (n.)
break the law
completely
counterfeiter
equipment*
fake (adj.)
illegal*
ink (n.)
nervous
prevent
scanner
technology*

UNIT 4

annoyed
block (v.)
blow your nose
civilized
confused
elderly
enforce*
etiquette
expert (n.)*
make eye contact with
manners
pole (n.)
push (v.)
rely on*
rude
sneeze (v.)

UNIT 5

allergic

approve

benefits*

complex*

diet (n.)

environment*

ethical

food chain

grains

insects

population

resist

weed (n.)

UNIT 6

adventure

affect (v.)*

dangerous

defeat (v.)

fail

intelligence*

journey (n.)

magic

mentor (n.)

opportunity

protect

safety

struggle (v.)

succeed

treasure (n.)

UNIT 7

antibiotic

bandage

blood

cure (v.)

fever

flow (n.)

gently

patient (n.)

popular

relax*

saliva

shot (n.)

sore throat

swelling

swollen

treat (v.)

vein

UNIT 8

adapt*

ancestors

connected

convince*

destroy

endangered

holy

nomadic

powerful

protest (v.)

roots

settled

survive*

unique*

TEXT CREDITS

UNIT 8

Map from Wade Davis, "The issue is whether ancient cultures will be able to change on their own terms," *National Geographic,* August 1999. Vol 196, No2. p. 62–89. Ngs Maps/National Geographic Stock. Reprinted by permission. (188)

"Will Indigenous Cultures Survive?" E. Davis/National Geographic Stock. Reprinted by permission. (191,192)

Based Upon "Write a Letter for the Penan" from *Survival for Tribal Peoples,* http://www.survivalinternational.org/actnow/writealetter/penan. Courtesy of Survival International. (195,196)

PHOTO CREDITS

Cover photo credits: (top left) Comstock Images/Getty Images, (top right) al1center/Fotolia, (middle) Lou Linwei/Alamy, (bottom left) Hill Street Studios/Blend Images/Corbis, (bottom right) monika3steps/Shutterstock.

Page xii (top) Voice of America; p. 2 Ken Seet/Corbis; p. 6 Andres Rodriguez/Fotolia; p. 10 elkor/E+/Getty Images; p. 11 (top) Diana Nguyen/MCT/Newscom, (bottom) Speedfighter/Fotolia; p. 26 AFP/Getty Images; p. 30 Rob Rich/Everett Collection/Newscom; p. 34 James Boardman/Alamy; p. 35 Hill Street Studios/Blend Images/Corbis; p. 41 (top) arekmalang/Fotolia, (bottom) michaeljung/Fotolia; p. 54 digitalreflections/Shutterstock; p. 58 ExQuisine/Fotolia; p. 80 Friedrich Stark/Alamy; p. 82 (top left) Arcady/Shutterstock, (top middle) Arcady/Shutterstock, (top right) RAYphotographer/Shutterstock, (bottom) Stan Tess/Alamy; p. 88 (top) nyul/Fotolia, (bottom) Horizons WWP/Alamy; p. 89 (top) Luciano Lepre/Glow Images, (bottom) Brennan Bill/Perspectives/Getty Images; p. 93 nyul/Fotolia; p. 106 Image Source/Alamy; p. 108 Pakhnyushcha/Shutterstock; p. 110 (left) Jeff J Mitchell/Getty Images, (right) Adam Gault/OJO Images RF/Getty Images; p. 111 (left) Andia/Alamy, (right) anat chant/Shutterstock; p. 115 (top) Elena Shashkina/Shutterstock, (bottom) marco mayer/Shutterstock; p. 132 Bastian Kienitz/Alamy; p. 134 KC Hunter/Alamy; p. 139 (top) Andrey_Arkusha/Fotolia, (bottom) Lajos Soos/AP Images; p. 145 KOMPASstudio/Shutterstock; p. 158 pat_hastings/Fotolia; p. 163 sydeen/Shutterstock; p. 167 Roger de la Harpe/SuperStock; p. 186 Lou Linwei/Alamy; p. 191 Maria Stenzel/National Geographic Creative/Getty Images; p. 195 Reinhard Dirscherl/Alamy; p. 206 STR/epa/Corbis; p. 209 Robert Harding Picture Library Ltd/Alamy.

THE PHONETIC ALPHABET

Consonant Symbols

/b/	be	/t/	to
/d/	do	/v/	van
/f/	father	/w/	will
/g/	get	/y/	yes
/h/	he	/z/	zoo, busy
/k/	keep, can	/θ/	thanks
/l/	let	/ð/	then
/m/	may	/ʃ/	she
/n/	no	/ʒ/	vision, Asia
/p/	pen	/tʃ/	child
/r/	rain	/dʒ/	join
/s/	so, circle	/ŋ/	long

Vowel Symbols

/ɑ/	far, hot	/iy/	we, mean, feet
/ɛ/	met, said	/ey/	day, late, rain
/ɔ/	tall, bought	/ow/	go, low, coat
/ə/	son, under	/uw/	too, blue
/æ/	cat	/ay/	time, buy
/ɪ/	ship	/aw/	house, now
/ʊ/	good, could, put	/oy/	boy, coin